JUDICIAL REVIEW

AND

CONSTITUTIONAL POLITICS

Other Titles in this Series:

JUDICIAL REVIEW AND CONSTITUTIONAL POLITICS

by **Keith E. Whittington**

**Published by the
American Historical Association
400 A Street, SE
Washington, DC 20003
www.historians.org**

**and sponsored by the
Institute for Constitutional History
at the New-York Historical Society
and the George Washington University Law School**

ABOUT THE AUTHOR

KEITH E. WHITTINGTON is the William Nelson Cromwell Professor of Politics at Princeton University. His books include *Constitutional Construction: Divided Powers and Constitutional Meaning*; *Constitutional Interpretation: Textual Meaning, Original Intent, and Judicial Review*; *Political Foundations of Judicial Supremacy: The Presidency, the Supreme Court, and Constitutional Leadership in U.S. History*, and (with Howard Gillman and Mark A. Graber) the multi-volume *American Constitutionalism*.

The New Essays on American Constitutional History series is also sponsored by the Institute for Constitutional History at the New-York Historical Society and the George Washington University Law School.

© 2015 by the American Historical Association
ISBN: 978-0-87229-218-5

Published in 2015 by the American Historical Association. As publisher, the American Historical Association does not adopt official views on any field of history and does not necessarily agree or disagree with the views expressed in this book.

Library of Congress Cataloging-in-Publication Data

Whittington, Keith E., author.
    Judicial review and constitutional politics / by Keith E. Whittington.
        pages cm -- (New essays on American constitutional history.)
    Includes bibliographical references.
    ISBN 978-0-87229-218-5 (pbk.)
    1. Judicial review—United States. 2. Constitutional law—United States. 3. Political questions and judicial power—United States. I. Title.
        KF4575.W47 2015
        347.73'12--dc23   2015030404

TABLE OF CONTENTS

SERIES INTRODUCTION

New Essays on American Constitutional History is published by the American Historical Association, in association with the Institute for Constitutional Studies. This series follows the lead of its predecessor, the Bicentennial Essays on the Constitution, published by the AHA under the editorship of Herman Belz as part of the commemoration of the two hundredth anniversary of the Constitution over two decades ago. The goal remains the same. The essays are intended to provide both students and teachers with brief, accessible, and reliable introductions to some of the most important aspects of American constitutional development. The essays reflect the leading scholarship in the field and address topics that are classic, timely, and always important.

American constitutionalism is characterized by a series of tensions. Such tensions are persistent features of American constitutional history, and they make a frequent appearance in these essays. The American tradition emphasizes the importance of written constitutions. The United States Constitution declares that "this Constitution" is the "supreme law of the land." But time moves on. Politics and society are ever changing. How do we manage the tension between being faithful to a written constitutional text and adapting to changing political circumstances? To the extent that the American brand of constitutionalism binds us to the past, creates stability, and slows political change, how do we balance these conservative forces with the pressures of the moment that might demand departures from inherited ways of doing things and old ideas about rights and values? We sometimes change the terms of the old text through amendment or wholesale replacement of one constitution with another (from the Articles of Confederation to the Constitution at the national level, or more often at the state level), but we apply and adapt the inherited constitutional text through interpretation and practice. All the while, we manage the tension between being faithful to the text that we have and embracing the "living constitution" that grows out of that text.

Law figures prominently in the American constitutional tradition. Our written constitutions are understood to be fundamental laws and part of our legal code. They are the foundation of our legal system and superior to all other laws. They provide legally enforceable rules for judges and others to follow. Judges and lawyers play an important role in interpreting American constitutions and translating the bare bones of the original text into the detailed body of doctrine known as constitutional law. It has often been the dream of judges, lawyers, and legal scholars to insulate constitutional law from the world of politics. There is a long-held aspiration for judges and lawyers to be able to spin out constitutional law in accord with established principles of justice, reason, and tradition. But politics has also been central to the history of American constitutionalism. Constitutions are created by political actors and serve political purposes. Once in place, constitutional rules and values are politically contested, and they are interpreted and put into practice by politicians and political activists, as well as by judges. The tension between law and politics is a persistent one in American constitutional history.

A final tension of note has been between power and liberty. In the modern tradition, constitutional government is limited government. Constitutions impose limits and create mechanisms for making those constraints effective. They specify what the boundaries of government power are and what rights individuals and groups have against government. But there is also an older tradition, in which constitutions organize and empower government. The U.S. Constitution contains both elements. Many of its provisions, especially the amendments, limit government. These are some of the most celebrated features of the Constitution, and they have become the basis for much of the constitutional law that has been developed by the judiciary. But the Constitution was specifically adopted to empower the federal government and create new, better institutions that could accomplish national objectives. Both the U.S. Constitution and the state constitutions are designed to gather and direct government power to advance the public good. Throughout American constitutional history, judges, politicians, and activists have struggled over the proper balance between empowering government and limiting government and over the best understanding of the rights of individuals and the public welfare.

These essays examine American constitutionalism, not a particular constitutional text. The U.S. Constitution figures prominently in these essays, as it does in American history, but the American constitutional tradition includes other foundational documents, including notably the state constitutions. These texts are a guide to the subject matter of these essays, but they are not exhaustive of it. Laws, court decisions, administrative actions, and custom, along with founding documents, perform constitutional functions in the American political system, just as they do in the British system where there is no single written "constitution." Whether "written" or "unwritten," constitutions perform certain common tasks.

Constitutions define the organic structures of government, specifying the basic institutions for making and implementing public policy, including the processes for altering the constitution itself. Constitutions distribute powers among those institutions of government, delegating, enumerating, prohibiting, and reserving powers to each governmental body. The flip side of entrusting power and discretion to governmental bodies is the definition of limits on those powers, the specification of individual and collective rights. Constitutions also specify who participates in the institutions of government and how and to whom the power of government applies. That is, constitutions identify the structures of citizenship and political jurisdiction. Across its seven articles and twenty-seven amendments, the U.S. Constitution addresses all of these topics, but the text is only a starting point. These topics form the subject matter of New Essays on American Constitutional History.

Writing early in the twentieth century, the great constitutional historian Edward Corwin observed that relatively few citizens actually read the U.S. Constitution, despite its brevity. He thought that this was in part because the "real constitution of the United States has come to mean something very different from the document" itself. The document laid out the framework of government, but "the real scope of the powers which it should exercise and of the rights which it should guarantee was left, to a very great extent, for future developments to determine." Understanding American constitutionalism requires understanding American constitutional history. It is a history of contestation and change, creation and elaboration. These essays aim to illuminate that history.

—*Keith E. Whittington,*
Princeton University

—*Gerry Leonard,*
Boston University School of Law

INTRODUCTION

J udicial review is an American innovation. The availability of constitutional review of legislation has now become commonplace, so much so
that countries that do not empower courts to invalidate laws now have
their credentials as constitutional democracies called into question. Even
England, the birthplace of both parliamentary sovereignty and many of the
civil liberties that Americans take for granted, has been under pressure to
adopt a legally enforceable bill of rights and empower courts to strike down
statutes. But for much of its history, the United States stood nearly alone in
its acceptance of this exceptional institution.

The embrace of a power of constitutional review did not come easily
to other constitutional systems. American-style judicial review was
self-consciously rejected by many constitutional reformers in other parts
of the world. For them, judicial review was not necessary to, and perhaps
not even compatible with, the security of democracy and constitutional
liberties. The situation did not change until well into the twentieth century
when the Austrian legal theorist Hans Kelsen designed a form of constitutional review that won greater favor among Europeans. For the most part,
this Kelsian model of constitutional review is the one that has been copied
across the globe, not American-style judicial review. As European countries
reexamined their constitutional systems after World War II and new nations
gained their independence or democratized, they became convinced that
legislative acts should be subjected to constitutional scrutiny by independent
arbiters, but they generally found the Kelsian model to be a more attractive
means for achieving that goal.

Judicial review is the practice by which courts interpret the Constitution,
evaluate the constitutionality of statutes or particular applications of
statutes, and declare statutes that conflict with the Constitution to
be legally void, invalid, and unenforceable to the extent of the conflict.
The practice also extends to evaluating the actions of other government
officials—executives and judges—to determine whether those actions
comply with constitutional requirements. When exercising the power of
judicial review, courts are assessing the validity of government actions. The
courts may either strike down a statute as unconstitutional or uphold it
as consistent with constitutional mandates. Throughout American history,

courts have primarily upheld statutes against constitutional challenges. In doing so, they not only sustain government policies and help legitimate them, but they also articulate what the constitutional rules are that should guide political behavior. The courts do not just block legislation. They also channel and encourage legislative activity by indicating which paths are open to the government to follow and which paths are less accessible.

Constitutional review comes in many forms. Judicial review may be vertical or horizontal. Vertical judicial review involves court review of the actions of a subordinate government (e.g., federal review of a state legislature). Horizontal judicial review involves court review of a coordinate branch of the same government (e.g., state review of a state legislature). Judicial review may be centralized or decentralized. Centralized judicial review limits the power of review to a single, specialized court. Decentralized judicial review authorizes any judge to engage in constitutional interpretation. Judicial review may be concrete or abstract. Concrete judicial review occurs in the context of actual cases or controversies within the normal operation of the legal system. Abstract judicial review occurs before laws are implemented, or even before they are formally adopted. Judicial review may be hard or soft. Hard judicial review empowers courts to invalidate statutes and render them null and void, legally unenforceable. Soft judicial review only empowers courts to evaluate the constitutionality of statutes, but not to take action to hinder their implementation and enforcement.

American-style judicial review is a form of hard, decentralized, and (generally) concrete judicial review. Every judge in the United States may evaluate the constitutionality of a statute and declare unconstitutional laws to be void, but they may only do so when the constitutional question comes before them as part of the normal litigation process. American judges are generally not supposed to issue what are known as "advisory opinions," statements made outside of an existing case or controversy about the constitutionality of a proposed government action. Elaborate rules have been developed and changed over time by the courts specifying when constitutional questions have met this case-or-controversy requirement and are therefore justiciable. American courts do not accept hypothetical questions posed to them. Constitutional questions must be raised in litigation between adversarial parties who have suffered an identifiable legal injury that can be remedied by the courts. The federal courts spend more time engaging in vertical judicial review than horizontal judicial review, and the ability of the federal courts to supervise the actions of state governments and insure that the latter comply with the requirements of the U.S. Constitution was a major motivation for establishing the power of judicial review in the first place. Nonetheless, American courts are not limited to vertical judicial review and routinely evaluate the actions of their coordinate branches.

The Kelsian model of constitutional review popular elsewhere modifies many of these features that are characteristic of American-style judicial review. Systems based on this model routinely adopt centralized and abstract forms of review. The centralized model allows for the creation of a specialized constitutional court that is separate from the ordinary judiciary. In many countries, the judiciary is organized as a kind of bureaucratic civil service. A centralized model of judicial review keeps the power of evaluating the constitutionality of legislation from such civil servants and from individual, local magistrates. By contrast with a decentralized system, a single constitutional court consolidates all constitutional disputes in one place and allows for the possibility that those constitutional judges can have a different mode of selection and term of office. Many constitutional drafters objected to the idea that a single, local judge might obstruct the work of a national legislative assembly or that ordinary judges trained to resolve routine civil and criminal disputes would be called upon to address fundamental constitutional questions. Constitutional judges in Kelsian systems are often selected through a more political process, drawn from a pool of constitutional experts and political elder statesmen, and sit for limited terms of office. Kelsian constitutional courts often exercise forms of abstract constitutional review. Such courts do not ordinarily hear constitutional questions that arise as part of an ordinary legal case. Instead, constitutional questions are specially referenced to the constitutional court, which considers them in the abstract without consideration of the facts of any particular situation or in light of the implementation of the statute. Abstract constitutional review, therefore, more closely resembles the presidential veto in the American constitutional system, but with the only available grounds for invalidation being unconstitutionality. Standing to bring questions to constitutional courts may be highly restricted or dispersed widely. In some systems, only government leaders may ask the constitutional court to evaluate the constitutionality of a proposed statute. In others, any citizen might send a request that the court take up a constitutional question.

Constitutional review by courts is one way to try to ensure that constitutional requirements are respected and maintained by government officials, but judicial review is limited in its effect. Constitutional enforcement is a challenging problem for any political system. A constitutional drafter can write constitutional rules but cannot guarantee that those rules will be followed by government officials. If later government officials or the citizenry wish to depart from constitutional rules, constitutional drafters are in no position to stop them. Judicial review provides one mechanism for enforcing constitutional rules, but judges are inevitably embedded in a larger political and social context and are not necessarily able to secure compliance with unpopular constitutional commitments. For some, this fact has been comforting. Alexander Hamilton tried to reassure the opponents of the ratification of the United States Constitution by observing that the judiciary would be the "least dangerous branch," ringed by checks and balances that would limit what judges could do.[1] In the twentieth century, Justice Benjamin Cardozo reminded his readers that judges "do not stand aloof on these chill and distant heights. . . . The great tides and currents which engulf the rest of men do not turn aside in their course and pass the judges by."[2] For better or worse, then, judicial review is only a partial solution to the problem of constitutional maintenance.

Recent scholarship has emphasized the importance of politics in shaping constitutional understandings, practices, and law. "Popular constitutionalism" or the "Constitution outside the courts" has a variety of consequences for constitutional practice and for judicial review. Political practice is shaped directly by constitutional politics. Not only do judges enforce constitutional understandings by exercising the power of judicial review, but so do politicians, interest groups, and voters by using the tools available to them to insist that their ideas about constitutional meaning be put into practice. Elections, lobbying, and statutes are vehicles for enforcing constitutional rules, just as judicial review is. Politics also has consequences for how judicial review itself is exercised. Most immediately, ideas about constitutional meaning are debated in the political arena, and those ideas get translated into judicial opinions both directly (by influencing judges) and indirectly (by influencing the selection of judges). The history of constitutional maintenance is incomplete without an appreciation for the work of political actors who seek to shape constitutional practices and the effective meaning of the Constitution. And the history of judicial review is incomplete without an appreciation of how judges operate within a larger political system that both affects and is affected by judicial decisions.

Ever since the emergence of the Populists and Progressives at the turn of the twentieth century, the institution of judicial review has struggled with the charge that it is antidemocratic. Some Progressives like former president Theodore Roosevelt and Judge Learned Hand called for a "pure democracy" and questioned whether the country needed a "bevy of Platonic guardians" to run its affairs from the courthouse.[3] More recently, the legal philosopher Jeremy Waldron has emphasized the extent to which constitutional questions are inescapably subject to deep political disagreement and has asked why a handful of legal elites rather than democratic majorities should resolve them.[4] The power of the courts to strike down legislation inevitably leads to conflicts between judges, legislatures, and popular majorities. The courts have maintained and even expanded the power of judicial review over the course of American history despite these conflicts, but the tensions remain and the power of the courts is always subject to question and challenge by those who are constrained by their rulings. Political actors, scholars, and citizens are constantly engaged in a process of negotiating the fit between the power of judicial review and democratic sensibilities.

The essay has three objectives. First, it surveys the development of judicial review and the debates surrounding the practice. Second, it introduces some aspects of constitutional politics. Finally, it provides a brief review of the substantive development of constitutional law across American history.

I. Origins of Judicial Review in the United States

J udicial review was not born in a single moment. The practice evolved in fits and starts until it reached its current form. The ideas and politics supporting the emergence of judicial review can be traced along multiple paths, most of which extend to the period before the adoption of the U.S. Constitution. Even so, the very term "judicial review" as a name for the power to interpret the Constitution and invalidate statutes is of modern origin, having been coined in the early twentieth century. The relatively late coinage reflects the growing significance of the practice by the end of the nineteenth century.

The written constitutions of the United States—both federal and state constitutions—are distinctive in not being explicit about a power of judicial review. Most modern constitutions include explicit provisions accounting for a possible power of constitutional review, its form, and its limitations. The U.S. Constitution only hints at the possibility of judicial review.[5] This absence has opened the door to questions about the legitimacy of institution. Populists at the end of the nineteenth century questioned whether such a power had really been vested in courts by the U.S. Constitution or whether the U.S. Supreme Court had usurped the power to repeal statutes from the legislature and the people in the early nineteenth century. Such questions persisted among activists, politicians, and scholars well into the twentieth century. The idea that the power of judicial review was "established" by Chief Justice John Marshall in his opinion in *Marbury v. Madison* (1803) simultaneously suggested that Marshall had invented the power from thin air, and that the institution as experienced in the twentieth century had deep foundations in the wisdom of the Great Chief Justice.[6] In fact, John Marshall was a relative latecomer to establishing judicial review, but his actions and arguments were important to consolidating the institution in the early republic.

The roots of judicial review in the United States extend to the colonial period. The great English legal scholar William Blackstone was clear in describing the state of the British constitutional system in the eighteenth century. Parliament ruled supreme. The British constitution consisted of a diverse set of political customs, practices, and normative commitments that could be marshaled in political debate but that were ultimately mutable in the face of clear legislative action. English judges were charged with respecting the rights of those who came before them, but they were not empowered to invalidate or ignore statutory directives from Parliament.

Sir Edward Coke of the Court of Common Pleas had provided a glimpse into an alternative system in *Bonham's Case* (1610), but little came of it in England.[7] Parliament had empowered the College of Physicians to license, judge, and punish individuals who practiced medicine. The college tried and convicted Dr. Thomas Bonham of practicing medicine without a license, subjecting him to a fine and imprisonment. Coke held that the charter of the college did not in fact give it the power to punish those who practiced medicine without a license, but he went further and suggested that Parliament could not have given the college the power to serve as both accuser and judge in such a case. The "common law will control Acts of Parliament," and if necessary render the statute "void." Later English judges denounced the doctrine announced by Coke, and some have suggested Coke merely intended to say that the common law should shape how judges interpret statutory directives. Either way, *Bonham's Case* did not launch a practice of constitutional review in England. Parliament, not the courts, would have the final say over the validity of laws.

Coke's dicta won new life in the American colonies. During the Stamp Act Crisis in Boston, Massachusetts lawyer James Otis attempted to resuscitate *Bonham's Case* as a limit on parliamentary power. Otis argued in pamphlets and legal briefs that courts had the power to refuse to enforce unconstitutional statutes. In particular, the internal taxes that Parliament had imposed on the colonists and the general warrants that were being issued to assist custom agents in searching for contraband were, according to Otis, contrary with English liberties. The courts in Massachusetts, he contended, should declare these violations to be invalid. The colonial courts declined to follow what they regarded as an anarchic doctrine, and Otis and other colonial activists moved on to other arguments in the years leading up to the American Revolution. Otis provided a valuable suggestion that statutes could be unconstitutional and legally void, but most lawyers in the colonies and the early republic accepted Blackstone's view that no institution stood above Parliament within the British constitutional scheme.

But the American colonists were familiar with other arguments for the supremacy of constitutions over legislatures. Each North American colony was itself governed by a written charter, which served as a local constitution. The charters specified the powers, duties, and rights of the various officers in the colony, and they promised that the colonists would enjoy traditional English liberties and legal rights. Of course, none included a power of judicial review. Many of them did, however, include a power of imperial review. The Privy Council was a royal body charged with overseeing the colonies, among other tasks. The council acted as both the supreme appellate court for the colonial judiciaries and as an imperial supervisory body. Of particular note was the fact that colonial assemblies were required to send a copy of their legislative acts to the council for its review and approval. The council was authorized to veto colonial legislation that conflicted with broader imperial policy or that violated the colonial charters or rights of the colonists. In practice, the colonists often resented imperial oversight and took steps to obstruct the ability of the Privy Council to be effective auditors of local policymaking. Nonetheless, the council was active in evaluating, and vetoing, colonial statutes. The practice of Privy Council review thus created a visible reminder that charters controlled legislatures and provided a model for how constitutional constraints could be made effective.

The colonists also embraced political theories that emphasized the limits on government power. Blackstone contended that there was "no power in the ordinary forms of the constitution" above Parliament.[8] The colonists generally came to accept that description of the organization of the British government. They did not, however, accept the idea that parliamentary authority was unlimited. Near the end of the Stamp Act Crisis, Samuel Adams led the drafting of a circular letter adopted by the Massachusetts lower house that contended that "the supreme legislative derives its powers and authority from the constitution," and as a consequence the legislature "cannot overleap the bounds of it without destroying its own foundation." Allegiance and sovereignty were linked in the constitution, and a parliament that overstepped the limits of its sovereign authority could not demand the allegiance of its subjects. The requirement of consent before taxation was an "essential unalterable right in nature" that was in turn part of the "fundamental law" of the realm. The colonists claimed "this natural and constitutional right."[9] Thomas Paine captured revolutionary American thinking in asserting,

> A constitution is a thing *antecedent* to a government, and
> a government is only the creature of a constitution. . . .
> A constitution, therefore, is to a government, what the
> laws made afterwards by that government are to a court
> of judicature. The court of judicature does not make the
> laws, neither can it alter them; it only acts in conformity
> to the laws made: and the government is in like manner
> governed by the constitution.[10]

For the revolutionaries who were questioning the authority of the
British Parliament to continue its rule over North America, the appeal
to a higher law that trumped the mandates of government officials was
self-evident. If the authority of the legislature was contingent on the
compatibility of its statutes with the fundamental law, then finding more
effective mechanisms for defending those limits on legislative authority
was a natural next step. As Virginia jurist St. George Tucker argued in
annotating his popular American edition of Blackstone's treatise, in the
United States "absolute power is not delegated to the government: it
remains with the people, whose safety requires that the government which
they have themselves established, should be limited."[11] If the Constitution
is an act of the people, then the legislature could have no authority to alter
the Constitution or infringe upon it.

There are many ways of attempting to prevent and correct constitutional violations. Perhaps the most natural to the revolutionary
generation was the thought that the people themselves would safeguard
the constitution. If American constitutions were people's documents,
designed to delegate limited power to the government, then the people
could be expected to take an interest in whether their governors adhered
to the terms of the contract. A free press and frequent elections would
ensure that government abuses would be revealed and checked. The
people would rally to the defense of their rights. This vision depended
on a particular analysis of the problems that human freedom faced. The
British experience suggested that the primary threat to liberty came from
unaccountable, or insufficiently accountable, government officials. The
people would not oppress themselves, but independent powerholders
might oppress them. A properly constructed republic would keep political
leaders on a short leash, and the reins of power would be put in the hands
of those best positioned to act in the interest of liberty.

Government officials would also be obliged to adhere to constitutional
requirements. If the problem of British constitutionalism was that the
Parliament had ultimate authority over the terms of the constitution
itself, then the solution was to place the constitution over the government.

American political leaders could not alter the constitution through ordinary legislative processes, and so constitutional commitments made by the drafters could be expected to be more enduring. Still, as James Madison later noted, constitutional requirements could become mere "parchment barriers" if they did not line up with political incentives and preferences.[12] American legislatures may not have the authority to alter the constitution, but in practice they might well violate it with impunity. The solution that he and other constitutional drafters offered was to try to bring political incentives into alignment with constitutional features. Political ambition should be harnessed to goals of the constitutional drafters. Not only would government officials have a duty to maintain the constitution, but they would also find it in their interest to marshal constitutional arguments and defend constitutional prerogatives. In the language of modern political economists, constitutional arrangements will be most stable if they are "self-enforcing," enlightened self-interest running with, rather than counter to, constitutional rules and political actors seeing the promise of greater benefits from adhering to the constitution rather than breaking it.

Some early constitution-writers pondered new institutional devices that might help make good on constitutional guarantees. Perhaps the most famous was the council of censors. The 1776 Pennsylvania state constitution included a provision establishing an elected "Council of Censors." The council, which would be close to the size of a legislative assembly, would meet every seventeen years to "enquire whether the constitution has been preserved inviolate in every part." If necessary, the council could pass resolutions of censure, order impeachments, and recommend the repeal of statutes. The council did not itself have the power to repeal or void statutes. Inspired by classical Roman institutions, various republican writers of the eighteenth century were intrigued by the idea of such a council, and as the United States separated itself from Great Britain, some Americans thought such a council would provide a popular check on government abuses. The experiment was short-lived, however.

The Philadelphia Constitutional Convention in 1787 considered various proposals to check legislatures. James Madison was particularly concerned with providing a means for the national government to supervise the state governments. For Madison, the lack of state accountability to national commitments, from international treaties to constitutional rules, was among the most serious flaws of the first federal constitution, the Articles of Confederation. He strenuously argued that the new U.S. Constitution should contain a congressional veto over state laws. Others in Philadelphia were much less comfortable giving Congress that kind of potential power over the internal affairs of individual states, and the congressional veto proposal was defeated. Madison also suggested the creation of a "Council of Revision," which would consist of the president and a group of federal judges. The council would have the power to veto any bill proposed by Congress and every statute passed by a state legislature, subject only to a congressional override. This proposal was also defeated, though a version of the veto power over congressional bills was given to the president alone. These proposals did not confine the veto power to constitutional concerns. Congress or the Council of Revision would have possessed the power to reject any statute for any reason, but the desire to stop violations of the constitutional compact was a central concern driving these proposals.

Courts were a more natural vehicle for evaluating the constitutionality of statutes. Madison's favored policy of a national legislative veto over state laws was rejected by the Philadelphia Convention. Roger Sherman and Gouverneur Morris thought the congressional veto was "unnecessary, as the Courts of the States would not consider as valid any law contravening the Authority of the Union." Moreover, the federal courts could "set aside" constitutionally improper state laws, which could not after all be "valid and operative." Even Madison assumed that the federal judiciary could "set aside" state laws and that the state courts could enforce the terms of the federal Constitution, but he doubted that either would be as effective in advancing the national interest as a congressional veto. After the congressional veto was rejected by the convention delegates, Maryland's Luther Martin immediately proposed the core of what would eventually become the supremacy clause, which was agreed to without objection. The "Judiciaries of the several States" were to be "bound" by federal law and charged with implementing that law through their decisions. While objecting to a later proposal to give the president and the Supreme Court a joint veto over congressional bills, Martin made the assumption of a power of judicial review explicit, observing that "the Constitutionality of laws . . . will come before the Judges in their proper judicial character," where they already possessed the power to "negative" unconstitutional statutes. Given those judicial duties, involving the judges in the passage of legislation would be improper. Not everyone agreed on the value of a more general veto over "oppressive or pernicious" federal legislation, but none of the delegates appeared to have doubted that judges would at least have the duty and capacity to declare unconstitutional legislation "void."[13]

Once a constitution was recognized as law, and not merely a blueprint of government or set of political maxims, judicial interpretation and application followed naturally. Once a constitution was recognized as supreme law, sitting atop the legal hierarchy above mere statutes, judicial declarations invalidating legislation could be expected, if not necessarily welcomed.

II. Early Judicial Review

The state courts were initially more active than the federal courts, and the power of judicial review was launched fairly smoothly in some states. In 1782, the Virginia Court of Appeals struck down a wartime state law that purported to remove the governor's pardoning power.[14] The state attorney general admitted that the court possessed a power to declare laws in violation of the constitution to be void, and the justices used the occasion to explain the power of judicial review. There was little uproar over the claim to power, and in short order the court went on to declare other statutes to be constitutionally impermissible. By the time of John Marshall's appointment to the U.S. Supreme Court in 1800, judicial review was a well-established practice in his home state and was generally regarded as a natural implication of the revolutionary effort at constitution writing in America. Some other states likewise adopted judicial review without much difficulty. In the 1790s, the South Carolina high court struck down laws without incident. The New Jersey court was able to invalidate statutes with only some localized complaints.

In several other states, however, the actual practice of judicial review got off to a rocky start. In New Hampshire, the legislature debated for a year whether to impeach or otherwise sanction the judges of a county court for declaring unconstitutional a law transferring jurisdiction over small debts to justices of the peace. The judges were eventually vindicated when a legislative committee determined that the court's actions were constitutionally justified, and the legislature repealed the offensive statute. In Rhode Island, the judges of the high court were censured in a legislative resolution for invalidating a statute and were almost all replaced within a year. In North Carolina, the Supreme Court was reluctantly pushed into invalidating a statute involving the confiscation of Loyalist property, provoking protests and legislative sanction. Even the hint of judicial review in New York incited public protests and legislative censure. Courts in some other states, such as Massachusetts and Maryland, did not even issue any constitutional decisions until the nineteenth century.

Some of those examples were already in front of the delegates in Philadelphia by the time of the drafting of the U.S. Constitution in 1787, and the Federalists were active in promoting them. James Iredell had been an advocate in the North Carolina case, and was a leading Federalist in that state. He was not chosen to attend the Philadelphia Convention, however, and two of North Carolina's delegates had already expressed their hostility to the idea of judicial review in their own state. As part of his effort to support and encourage the North Carolina judges, Iredell (pseudonymously) penned one of the first published defenses of the power of judicial review. Iredell argued that Americans should embrace judicial review for precisely the same reason they had opposed parliamentary supremacy during the Revolution. The drafters of the state constitution had not intended to create a "despotic power" in the state legislature; the legislature was merely "a creature of the constitution" and had not legal authority to act beyond its terms. The courts could not, consistent with their own duty, give legal effect to putative statutes that attempted to alter the fundamental law of the state that had been laid by the people.[15] Alexander Hamilton, who served as a delegate for New York, had argued a key case before the New York high court contending that for a state to breach a treaty "is a violation of their constitution[al] authority." So long as the confederation remained in existence, he argued, "a law of a particular state derogating from its constitutional authority is no law," and state judges were obliged to give effect to the more fundamental law rather than to the state statute.[16] Hamilton built on those arguments in his canonical essay in the *Federalist Papers*. In Federalist No. 78, Hamilton emphasized that an independent judiciary "is peculiarly essential in a limited Constitution," where "certain specified exceptions to the legislative authority" were written down. Such constitutional constraints, Hamilton asserted, "can be preserved in practice no other way than through the medium of the courts of justice, whose duty it must be to declare all acts contrary to the manifest tenor of the Constitution void." Without this ability to declare unconstitutional laws legally void, constitutionally secured rights "would amount to nothing."

   The federal courts began to render constitutional decisions soon after they were established. In the 1790s, several federal circuit courts grappled with the problem of the Invalid Pensioners Act of 1792. The statute assigned to circuit court judges the task of certifying injured Revolutionary War veterans as qualified to receive a pension. From the legislature's perspective, the judges were the most convenient federal officials for meeting American citizens out in the countryside, given the undeveloped quality of the federal state. But the Constitution did not anticipate the possibility of assigning administrative duties to the judicial branch, and the circuit court judges struggled with the question of whether they should comply with these new statutory duties. Because there were no legal cases involving the statute, the judges could not take official action or issue an opinion in a case. Most instead chose to refuse to process the pension claims and to explain their constitutional objections to the law in formal letters to President Washington. Congress eventually took action to revise the statute so as to avoid the constitutional concerns. Federalists reacted with alarm at the possibility that the judges were undermining the authority of Congress, but the emerging Jeffersonian critics of the administration were hopeful that the courts might soon nullify more important policies, like the statute creating the Bank of the United States. Their hopes were misplaced, however, as demonstrated by the U.S. Supreme Court's upholding the power of Congress to impose a tax on the ownership of carriages in a closely watched test case.[17] A federal circuit court struck down in 1795 a state law attempting to arbitrate land claims, while providing the first explanation of the power of judicial review by a federal judge.[18] But more often, the federal courts upheld statutes against constitutional challenge, whether the carriage tax, the circumvention of jury trials when enforcing a trade embargo, the criminalization of criticism of the government, or a state law interfering with the probate of a will.[19] By the time of Jefferson's election in 1800, the federal courts had demonstrated their willingness to hear and decide constitutional challenges to state and federal laws, even if they had not shown much inclination toward invalidating statutes.

The Marshall Court brought the power of judicial review into greater prominence. John Marshall was a well-respected lawyer and politician in Virginia before briefly serving as secretary of state at the end of John Adams's presidency. His appointment to be chief justice of the United States by the lame-duck president set the stage for transforming the court. Marshall was the fourth person to serve as chief justice. Although the first three were eminent figures in the early republic (more so than Marshall at the time of his appointment), it was John Marshall who set himself the task of building the federal judiciary into an important branch of the federal government. Marshall no doubt benefitted from the slowly increasing stream of cases that entered the federal system over time, but he took maximum advantage of his opportunities. He proved well suited to the court, remaining in office for more than three decades, convincing his colleagues to subordinate themselves to a single opinion of the court, writing a majority of those opinions himself (and almost all of the opinions in constitutional cases), managing the small-scale politics of retaining leadership of the court even as the Jeffersonians replaced all of his Federalist colleagues, and navigating the large-scale politics of giving voice to his moderate Federalist constitutional values in a Jeffersonian era.

The first significant cases confronting Marshall arose out of the same partisan maneuvering that was threatening to cripple the federal courts.

With the national elections lost, the Federalists in 1800 sought to strengthen the federal judiciary. Congress finally endorsed a set of reforms long urged by nationalist friends of the courts, which gave the federal courts the jurisdiction to hear a broader range of cases, freed the Supreme Court justices from having to travel to sit with circuit judges to try cases and hear appeals, and incidentally created a large number of new judicial offices for President Adams to fill. Federal judges were already in bad odor with the Jeffersonians because of their enthusiastic enforcement of the 1798 sedition statute that jailed Republican editors and politicians, and the Judiciary Act of 1801 merely confirmed their belief that the federal courts were in the pocket of Federalist partisans. Among the first acts of the Jeffersonian Congress was a repeal of the Judiciary Act of 1801, thus putting the newly appointed judges out of their jobs. The House of Representatives quickly followed up by impeaching two of the worst offenders on the bench, including Associate Justice Samuel Chase (he was not convicted in the Senate).

Chief Justice John Marshall did not establish the power of judicial review, but his powerful opinion in the 1803 case of *Marbury v. Madison* would eventually become the symbol of it. William Marbury had been appointed to a minor judicial post in the District of Columbia at the end of the Adams administration. His nomination was confirmed by the Senate, and the commission was signed by the president, but his commission was among those that did not get delivered by Secretary of State John Marshall in the frantic last hours before Jefferson's inauguration. Jefferson believed that the appointment was not complete until the commission was signed, sealed, and delivered. He ordered his secretary of state, James Madison, to hold any remaining commissions until Jefferson had decided how those offices should be filled. The commission was the evidence of a judge's right to exercise the authority of office, and Marbury could not take his seat until the commission was delivered. The Federalists (probably including Marshall himself) convinced Marbury to file suit in Marshall's Supreme court to force a confrontation with the new president. By the time the case was heard, however, the political climate for the court did not favor a confrontation. The administration refused to even admit that a commission existed or that the court had jurisdiction to hear a case involving the internal operation of the executive branch. No lawyers were sent to defend the White House or provide arguments on why Marbury should not receive his commission.

For nearly a hundred years, Marshall's discussion of the power of judicial review at the end of his opinion in *Marbury* was not regarded as the most important feature of the case. Most of Marshall's opinion was dedicated to explaining why Marbury had a legal right to his commission, why the courts had the authority to vindicate that right, and what the constitutional scope of the Supreme Court's jurisdiction might be. On those subjects, Marshall was emphatic. Having been nominated and confirmed, Marbury was legally entitled to his office. The administration had violated Marbury's rights, Marshall argued, and the courts were empowered to vindicate those rights even if it required issuing orders to executive officials. Cabinet officials did not have discretion to refuse to carry out their legal obligations, in this case to deliver a commission.

Having gone that far in his vigorous denunciation of the White House, Marshall needed an escape hatch. If the court ordered Madison to deliver the commission, the administration was likely to refuse to comply and demonstrate that the court was a toothless tiger. The solution was to strike down a minor provision of the Judicial Act of 1789 that arguably provided the grounding for Marbury's filing before the court. After adopting a somewhat questionable interpretation of the statutory provision, Marshall concluded that it exceeded the reach of Congress's authority to determine which cases could be first heard in the Supreme Court (the court's "original jurisdiction"). And here Marshall argued that the court could not follow the directions of Congress when Congress purported to do things that were not allowed by the text of the Constitution. If the court were to follow its own duty to obey the terms of the Constitution, it must refuse to give effect to contrary statutes, instead declaring them legally null and void. Marshall's argument was not innovative, but his language on the importance of a limited constitution was resonant with commonly held beliefs. The Jeffersonians railed at Marshall's critique of the administration's actions, but no one objected to his elaboration of the power of judicial review. Marshall issued no orders for the administration to ignore, and Marbury's term of office expired without his ever receiving a commission.

Perhaps more consequential than *Marbury* was the decision handed down a week later in *Stuart v. Laird. Stuart* involved a challenge to the controversial Jeffersonian repeal of the Judiciary Act of 1801. The case involved an aggrieved litigant rather than a displaced circuit court judge, but the suit provided an opportunity for the Supreme Court to declare the repeal to be invalid and reinstate the judicial reform (and Federalist court-packing) of 1801. The chief justice chose not to write the opinion for the court in *Stuart*, and the result was a brief statement dismissing the suit and avoiding the substantive issues. The repeal would stand, and the court would not pick a fight it would lose with the Jeffersonians.

Over the next three decades, the court would issue a number of important constitutional decisions, while carefully refraining from antagonizing the other two branches of the federal government. In the early nineteenth century, the court followed the pattern of the federal judiciary in the late eighteenth century, although increasing the pace at which cases were decided. The Marshall Court found occasion to strike down state laws, but generally upheld federal statutes against constitutional challenge. These state cases were sometimes of political importance.

The court struck down its first state law as violating the federal Constitution in *Fletcher v. Peck* in 1810. The case involved the Yazoo land scandal, in which nearly every member of the Georgia legislature accepted bribes to sell off vast tracts of public land to a group of land speculators. When the voters threw the rascals out, the newly elected legislature ostentatiously repealed the land grant and declared all the purchases void. By then, however, many tracts of land had already been sold to third parties. Over time, the effort to unravel the affair involved many of the most prominent lawyers and politicians in the country and a federal bailout. The specific lawsuit heard by the court was designed to settle the question of whether the repeal was valid. The legal basis for rejecting the repeal was less than clear, but many lawyers agreed there must be something wrong with a legislature reneging on its own land grants. The court concluded that the repeal act violated the constitutional prohibition on states impairing the obligations of contracts. In doing so, the court emphasized that the government's own grants were to be understood as contracts and that statutes undermining such grants were a violation of constitutionally protected property rights. Within a decade, the court further declared that corporate charters granted by the government were contracts that could not be altered by later legislatures. Such cases laid the groundwork for decades of litigation challenging not only statutes that interfered with contracts between private parties but also laws altering property interests arising from actions of the state.

The court laid down another constitutional marker against the states in limiting their authority to regulate interstate commerce. The Constitution grants Congress the power to regulate commerce among the several states, but states too continued to regulate some economic activity that crossed state lines. In the 1824 case of *Gibbons v. Ogden*, the court followed the suggestion of the Jeffersonian attorney general in holding that New York could not establish a monopoly over steamship traffic between New York and New Jersey. The court stretched to identify a federal statute that might conflict with New York's grant, allowing the justices to emphasize the supremacy of congressional power in regulating interstate commerce. Hovering in the background, however, was the possibility that states were simply barred from interfering with interstate commerce, regardless of whether Congress had acted. The court would not embrace that implication of the interstate commerce clause until after the Civil War. In the meantime, the jurisprudential concern was with the limits on state regulatory action rather than the scope of congressional power.

The court's supervision of the states was generally welcomed by national political officials, but it did not go unchallenged. At the extreme, states might simply ignore the court, as Georgia did when the justices in 1832 claimed jurisdiction over the state's criminal prosecution of individuals on tribal land within the boundaries of the state.[20] In such instances, the states claimed that their reserved police powers (the power to protect the health, safety, and welfare of their citizens) and inherent sovereign rights of self-protection imposed limits on how the federal government could interfere with state policies. A different kind of challenge came from Virginia, where the staunch Jeffersonian judge Spencer Roane in 1815 questioned the constitutionality of Section 25 of the Judiciary Act of 1789, which allowed appeals from state supreme courts to the U.S. Supreme Court in a limited set of cases. In a back-and-forth exchange between Roane on the one side and Marshall and Justice Joseph Story on the other, the U.S. Supreme Court declared that it must be the ultimate interpreter of the meaning of the U.S. Constitution and federal statutes. The court emphasized the value of national uniformity in legal expectations, but the suggestion that state judges could not be trusted to play fair with federal laws was clear.

The Marshall court was sometimes able to combine invalidating state laws with upholding federal laws. Most notably, the 1819 case of *McCulloch v. Maryland* upheld the congressional authority to charter a national bank, allowing Marshall to articulate an expansive understanding of the necessary and proper clause. Echoing nationalist arguments from Alexander Hamilton through Daniel Webster, the chief justice concluded, "Let the end be legitimate, let it be within the scope of the constitution, and all means which are appropriate, which are plainly adapted to that end, which are not prohibited, but consistent with the letter and spirit of the constitution, are constitutional." By 1819, however, few were overly concerned about the congressional power to charter a bank. Even James Madison, a leading critic of the First Bank of the United States advocated by Alexander Hamilton, had as president signed the law chartering the Second Bank in 1816. The contentious issue at stake in *McCulloch* was whether states could tax the bank. In some cases, states were actively seeking to drive branches of the bank out of their borders. In others, the states were merely trying to level the playing field between state-chartered and federally chartered banks and help fill their own depleted state treasuries. Regardless, Marshall intoned that "the power to tax involves the power to destroy," creating a broad doctrine that instrumentalities of the federal government had to be immune from state taxes.

The development of the power of judicial review in the early republic was an extended process with many players. When explaining the power of judicial review, judges and lawyers were as likely to cite Alexander Hamilton's influential contribution to the *Federalist Papers* as John Marshall's opinion in *Marbury*. Justice William Paterson's early constitutional opinion on property rights while riding circuit and the exchange between Justice Samuel Chase and Justice James Iredell over the meaning of the constitutional restriction on ex post facto laws were crucial in asserting the authority of the federal courts to evaluate the constitutionality of state laws.[21] State judges struggled to assert their authority to interpret the state constitutions and set aside conflicting legislative acts.

Judges succeeded in establishing their authority to enforce constitutional rules because they were generally working with, rather than working against, powerful political actors. Nationalists wanted courts to be able to fight the centrifugal forces of the federation. Jeffersonians wanted courts to be able to resist the abuses of Congress. Federalists wanted the courts to be able to resist the abuses of state legislatures. In an era that embraced constitutional checks and balances as a central part of republican government, an institution like judicial review was readily accepted as just another means for preserving public liberty against the possible abuses of public power.

III. SLAVERY AND WAR

The political and constitutional world looked very different in the 1830s and 1840s than it did in the first years of the republic. The last veteran of the Revolutionary War to serve as president left the White House in 1824. Chief Justice John Marshall's departure from the court in 1835 left it in the hands of men who had all come of age after the nation had declared its independence. The last surviving member of the Philadelphia Constitutional Convention, James Madison, passed away in 1836. By 1837, half the states had joined the Union after the ratification of the U.S. Constitution. The issues and divisions that had moved politics in the Washington administration had been upended by the War of 1812, western expansion, immigration, and the Era of Good Feelings. Throughout the country, conventions drafted new state constitutions that expanded the franchise and the power of the electorate while imposing new limits on legislative discretion. Mass political parties and interest groups emerged to mobilize the people around new leaders and new issues.

Among the constitutional changes wrought in many of those states was the shift from appointed to elected judiciaries. Appointed judges were too often seen as political cronies unwilling to make life difficult for their friends in the rest of the government. Judges elected directly by the people promised to be more independent of the politicians. Those hopes were soon realized, as elected judges armed with more constitutional restrictions began to invalidate statutes at a higher rate. Many of those cases reflected the growing distrust of legislative involvement with the economy. Many state legislatures had courted financial insolvency by heavily investing public funds and public credit in ill-fated schemes to build roads, canals, and railways. Judges began to more often apply constitutional limitations on how the legislatures could engage in economic development. In 1831, for example, the New York state court allowed the legislature to authorize a railroad to exercise the power of eminent domain so long as the land transfer served "the public interest." A decade later, the same court objected to a legislative program allowing builders of private roads to exercise the power of eminent domain as an unwarranted "attack" on the rights of private property.[22]

Jacksonian-era state courts laid down the markers for one of the key developments in constitutional jurisprudence in nineteenth century, the skepticism of "class legislation." Laws that tended to benefit or burden one part of society without being necessary to advance the common good were understood to be disfavored class legislation. Judges increasingly emphasized that such statutes were an abuse of the legislative power, in that they served private interests rather than any legitimate public interest. Such doctrinal developments built on earlier common law concepts that justified government action by reference to the public good, founding-era fears of factional (or special interest) politics, and Jacksonian fears of "monopoly" (the creation of special privileges through government action). Although often framed as a general background principle that delimited the legislative power granted by constitutions, the problem of public purposes and class legislation could also find a textual home in the "due process" or "law of the land" provisions of constitutions. As the Tennessee high court influentially declared when striking down a state law that sought to discriminate between suits filed on behalf of Native American land claims and other, similarly situated suits, the "'law of the land,' means a general public law, equally binding upon every member of the community." Statutes must create a general law that affected "the whole community equally"; "partial" or "private" law was void.[23]

Such arguments also informed judicial resistance to one of the major products of the culture wars of the period: alcohol prohibition. The temperance movement flourished in the antebellum years. A growing evangelical movement helped feed activism in a range of social reform efforts, from abolitionism to anti-gambling to temperance. Protestant evangelical-ism converged with nativist sentiment that was hostile to Catholic, and purportedly hard-drinking, immigrants. When efforts at moral suasion failed, temperance advocates turned to legal regulation of alcohol. The most extreme statutes prohibited individuals from selling, or keeping for purposes of sale, intoxicating liquors. Tavern owners and distilleries protested that such laws violated property rights by extinguishing the value of private property and issuing a blanket legislative declaration that an individual's property was contraband and a public nuisance without a judicial hearing to determine whether any particular stock of property caused public harm. State courts divided over how to treat this legislative innovation. The New York court spoke for some in worrying that if the legislature could by fiat forbid a formerly entirely legal class of property, then "there is no limitation upon the absolute discretion of the legislature, and the guarantees of the constitution are a mere waste of words." The legislature could regulate the trade in liquor, but it was outside the scope of legislative authority to simply declare that some class of property was "worthless and pernicious" and thus subject to government seizure. Property could only be forfeited if it was used in violation of the existing law, the law under which the property had been acquired in the first place, as determined by a neutral tribunal, just as life and liberty could be restricted only upon a showing that an individual had done something to forfeit his or her right to it.[24]

Such questions were not yet on the radar of the federal courts. They were matters of state law and state constitutional rights and prohibitions. The federal courts did, however, encounter a few politically controversial state policies, often through the avenue of the interstate commerce clause. The justices were often deeply divided over how best to understand the commerce clause and the restrictions that it imposed on the states. Whether and how the interstate slave trade might be regulated lurked behind the 1841 case of *Groves v. Slaughter*, which involved a state constitutional provision prohibiting the importation of slaves for sale. The problem of slavery was only a bit further in the background in other cases that involved policies that were controversial in their own right. The court narrowly upheld state liquor license requirements, but rejected the imposition of state taxes on ships carrying impecunious alien passengers. The court finally brought some order to its commerce clause jurisprudence in *Cooley v. Board of Wardens of the Port of Philadelphia*, concluding that objects "in their nature national" and requiring uniform regulations were beyond state control but leaving space for the states to exercise their police powers over matters that required local knowledge and variability.[25]

Slavery was at the center of the Supreme Court's most high-profile constitutional decisions involving federal statutes. Sometimes this involved upholding federal statutes against constitutional challenge, as was the case with the controversial fugitive slave law. Most significantly, Justice Joseph Story took the lead for the court in explaining the constitutionality of the Fugitive Slave Act of 1793 and attempting to turn back rising antislavery agitation.[26] The antislavery movement was strongest in Story's own New England, but the justice shared the nationalist sensibility of such "Cotton" Whigs as Daniel Webster who were willing to compromise with the slave interests in order to maintain union and advance favored economic policies. The court felt the need to rehearse those arguments in subsequent cases reaffirming the congressional power to override state laws regulating the detention and return of alleged fugitive slaves (including the northern personal liberty laws designed to obstruct the work of the slave catchers).[27]

Of course, in one infamous instance the court struck down a federal statue limiting slaveholding rights.[28] The background of the slave Dred Scott's suit for freedom is complex, and the court was initially inclined to send the case back to the states with a minimalist ruling. But the justices could not agree to maintain their silence in the face of the growing controversy over slavery.

The crux of Dred Scott's case turned on his residence in federal territory where slavery had been prohibited by the Missouri Compromise of 1820. One of the complications of the case was the question of whether Scott was entitled to claim federal jurisdiction for this particular suit, and here he relied on the diversity of state citizenship between himself and John Sanford. A bitterly divided court concluded that Congress did not have the constitutional authority to prohibit slave owners from carrying their slaves into a federal territory, while also arguing that Scott was not a citizen for purposes of diversity jurisdiction.[29] As with *Marbury*, the *Dred Scott* opinion indicated that the federal courts should not hear the case, and yet the court did not hesitate to speak to the merits of the dispute. Chief Justice Roger Taney hoped that a forceful opinion on the centrality of slavery to the constitutional scheme would help put down the Republican Party insurgency. Instead, Abraham Lincoln used the opinion as fire for his 1858 Illinois campaign for a seat in the U.S. Senate, which in turn propelled him to the head of the Republican Party. One of the dissenting justices, the Massachusetts Whig Benjamin Curtis, quit the court in disgust soon after *Dred Scott*, bitter at how he thought the chief justice had manipulated the publication of the opinions.

The U.S. Supreme Court upheld and invalidated federal statutes in other cases in the decades leading up to the Civil War, but most of those constitutional decisions were not of broad political significance.[30] Like the Marshall Court, the Taney Court often found itself on the sidelines as major constitutional controversies raged in the political arena. In part, the political parties had organized themselves to contest some of the most significant constitutional issues of the period. The founding generation was not comfortable with the idea of political parties, which reeked of disruptive factions. Political organizing was to be a temporary expedient, justifiable only until the constitutional apostates had been driven from the temple of government. The extinction of the Federalist Party might have vindicated those ideas. But it was not long before the victorious Jeffersonian Republicans splintered. The upstart New York politician Martin Van Buren took the lead in restoring and rationalizing a permanent two-party system. The Democratic Party, Van Buren argued, was the tool by which the people would articulate correct constitutional principles and enforce constitutional fidelity. Battling constitutional interpretations were central to party competition.[31] But the two major parties resolved not to fight each other over the slavery issue, leaving the major struggles over slavery to be fought within rather than between the parties.

In the years before the sectional crisis, the scope of federal power and separation of powers dominated the constitutional agenda of the period, and those issues were fought out between the parties, much more than in the courts. Henry Clay's "American System" of protective tariffs, internal improvements (infrastructure construction), and the Bank of the United States portended a dramatic centralization of power and was therefore anathema to the Jacksonian Democrats. Jacksonians challenged the constitutionality of each leg of the system. Jacksonian presidents vetoed internal improvement bills that did not serve sufficiently national purposes. States' rights southerners insisted that the congressional power to tax imports did not include a power to impose protectionist tariffs (that were damaging to the cotton economy, which depended on international trade).

Most notoriously, President Jackson fought to kill the Second Bank of the United States and prevent the chartering of a successor. Neither judicial precedents (such as John Marshall's opinion in *McCulloch*) nor political precedents (such as James Madison's acceptance of the Second Bank) deterred Jackson from arguing that the bank was unconstitutional. An issue that seemed settled two decades before was once again up in the air. Jackson's 1832 veto of the bill to recharter the bank established the Democratic orthodoxy of limited federal power. *McCulloch* was recognized as a dead letter by political observers of the day, but the Taney Court never had the opportunity to formally overturn it (even though there was almost certainly a majority of justices prepared to do so).[32] Jacksonian commitment and power within Congress and the White House ensured that the federal government did not adopt any policies in the decades before the Civil War that would have invited judicial reconsideration of *McCulloch*. Democratic political strength meant that a Democratic Court did not need to develop new constitutional law or explicitly repudiate the nationalist doctrines of the Marshall Court (or have much opportunity to do so).

The fight over the bank was also the occasion for the development of two competing views of presidential power. President Jackson exceeded all his predecessors in his proclivity for using the veto power, and he used it on more politically salient bills. From his veto of the construction of rival Henry Clay's Maysville Road to his veto of the bill rechartering the Bank of the United States, Jackson insisted on the president's right to challenge legislative judgments on federal policy. Whig leaders responded by asserting that presidents were constitutionally obliged to defer to legislative judgment. Succeeding Democratic presidents adhered to Jackson's views of the veto power, but Whigs continued to reject them. Whig president William Henry Harrison promised never to use the veto in a way that would "assist or control Congress . . . in its ordinary legislation."[33] When the Democratic-sympathizing John Tyler gained the Oval Office upon Harrison's death and once again exerted the veto power, former president John Quincy Adams drafted a House report calling for Tyler's impeachment and a constitutional amendment. The Whiggish argument for legislative supremacy did not fade away until after the Civil War.

President Jackson was willing to assert more than just the veto power in his assault on the bank. The successful veto of the rechartering bill blocked the extension of the bank, but it did not put an immediate end to the existing bank. The president's next step was to order the removal of all federal deposits from the bank. When Secretary of Treasury William Duane refused, Jackson dismissed him and appointed Roger Taney to serve as the acting secretary and carry out the president's wishes. Congressional Whigs were apoplectic. Jackson's actions raised two questions, whether the president could direct a cabinet member on how to perform his duties and whether the president could remove a cabinet member from office without regard to congressional preferences. For Jackson, the answer was obvious. The president's duty to take care that the laws be faithfully executed necessitated that all other executive officers be subordinate to his commands. Senate leader Henry Clay spearheaded passing resolutions of censure, arguing that Jackson was launching a "bloodless" revolution that would concentrate "all power in the hands of one man" and overturn the power of Congress to spread executive duties to "various responsible officers, checking and checked by each other."[34] When the Democrats retook the Senate majority in the 1834 elections, expunging the censure resolutions was among the first orders of business. The debate between Jackson's "unitary" theory of the executive and Clay's "pluralist" theory has continued off and on ever since.

The Civil War and Reconstruction raised a host of constitutional difficulties, few of which were addressed by the court. Secession itself was the first problem to be confronted. Many of the southern states claimed a constitutional right to voluntarily leave the Union. President James Buchanan contended that the secession ordinances were unconstitutional, but doubted that the federal government had the authority to do much about it. President Abraham Lincoln, by contrast, declared not only that secession was invalid but that the president of the United States was obligated to take necessary steps to prevent it.[35]

Taking action against the seceding states was itself constitutionally complicated. The government of the United States did not want to recognize the legitimate existence of the government of the Confederacy, though exercising the war powers against the Confederate nation would be straightforward. It was not clear that the federal government could declare or make war against the states. Lincoln's immediate solution was to characterize the Union's response as one of putting down a domestic rebellion while protecting federal property and loyal citizens from lawlessness. But this suggested that the federal government was engaged in a sort of police action, which rendered troubling such steps as the establishment of a naval blockade on southern ports. The Supreme Court quickly announced that "this Court must be governed by the decisions and acts of the political department of the Government," and concluded that Lincoln's actions were themselves "official and conclusive evidence to the court that a state of war existed" even if neither the Congress nor the president was empowered to declare war in such circumstances.[36]

The conduct of the war raised further delicate constitutional questions. Some involved questions of separation of powers. In the grips of the crisis, President Lincoln exercised unprecedented powers, from the first steps of launching the war effort (including the suspension of the writ of habeas corpus and the raising of federal troops) without calling Congress into session, to the steps needed to fight the war (including the emancipation of slaves within Confederate territory), to the process of ending the war (including the establishment of military governments in the conquered states). His successor, Andrew Johnson, continued this aggressive use of presidential power, from the use of mass pardons to shape the peace process, to the effort to declare the end of hostilities and restore civil government in the southern states, to the unilateral removal of executive officials who were not supportive of the president's initiatives. The former Democrat Johnson was less able to manage the Republicans in Congress than Lincoln had been, eventually resulting in his impeachment and isolation from policymaking.

Other questions involved the substantive limits on government power during a domestic war. A determined Congress and president pressed the limits of the Constitution by the passage of federal statutes allowing the confiscation of the property of supporters of the Confederacy (although the U.S. Supreme Court would not weigh in until well after the war had ended); military detentions of southern sympathizers (which the court only rejected after the war was over and most such prisoners had been released); and the adoption of the military draft (which state courts generally upheld but Roger Taney was prepared to strike down if an appropriate federal case had been filed). The Supreme Court and Congress combined to avoid judicial review of congressional Reconstruction and the maintenance of martial law in the southern states after the war, with the court declining to resolve cases that raised the issue and the legislature finally repealing the statutory jurisdiction that litigants needed to take cases to the Supreme Court. The court did strike down legal tender as a war measure that was no longer necessary and proper in peacetime, in an opinion written by Salmon Chase (who had administered the legal tender laws as Lincoln's secretary of treasury). Chase's slim majority immediately fell apart, however, when President U.S. Grant appointed two new justices and the reconstituted Court reversed course. The reversal avoided the potential financial nightmare of quickly returning to a gold standard, but invited a crisis of faith in political institutions that seemed to manipulate constitutional law so readily.

IV. The Administrative State and a National Economy

The end of Reconstruction marked the beginning of a new era in American constitutionalism. The Reconstruction Amendments reflected new concerns about democracy, as well as about the state governments. The experience of slavery and the political treatment of the freedmen raised new doubts about whether democratic majorities were more of a threat than a guardian of liberty, and new constitutional limits on the states invited unprecedented levels of judicial review of legislative decisions. That judicial intervention was more often aimed at economic conflict than racial conflict.[37] With the return of local (white) rule in the South, both national political parties turned their attention to managing economic development. Industrial capitalism and urbanization surged forward, leaving economic and social dislocation in their wake. The government responded with bold new policies. Meanwhile, the political parties fought close electoral contests, though sometimes over a narrow range of issues.

Over the next several decades, race relations were put on the back burner. Politically, the Democrats, with their electoral strength in the white South, were committed to white supremacy. Even the Republicans saw little to be gained by fighting battles on that front. The courts were generally willing to uphold the Jim Crow settlement that had been reached in the political arena. As Congress retreated, the U.S. Supreme Court imposed limits on how far the federal government could go to fight racial discrimination. Combating racial discrimination by private actors was ruled to be within the exclusive purview of the state governments. The federal government's flexibility in attempting to enforce racial equality in voting was curtailed. The court endorsed the view that laws requiring the separation of the races were consistent with the Fourteenth Amendment's guarantee of their "legal equality." The court gave only a few indications that there were significant constitutional answers to the most salient aspects of the race question. Courts pointed out that executive administrators had to operate under some legal standards so that arbitrary decisions, whether affecting racial minorities or others, could be prevented. Similarly, racial issues drove the U.S. Supreme Court to insist that state criminal proceedings meet a minimum threshold of fairness if they were to rise above mere lynch law. In 1917 the U.S. Supreme Court concluded that governments could not mandate residential segregation by restricting the rights of buyers and sellers of homes, but the significance of that decision was undermined to some degree by its subsequent decision to accept the legal validity of private racial covenants.[38]

In other contexts, judges, legal commentators, and social activists busily developed innovative rights claims, which tended to reflect new policies and social conditions. Thomas Cooley, one of the most influential state judges and treatise writers of the latter nineteenth century, cautioned,

> we think we shall find that general rules may sometimes be as obnoxious as special, when in their results they deprive parties of vested rights. While every man has a right to require that his own controversies shall be judged by the same rules which settle those of his neighbors, the whole community is also entitled at all times to demand the protection of the ancient principles which shield private rights against arbitrary interference, even though such interference may be under a rule impartial in its application. It is not the partial character of the rule, so much as its arbitrary and unusual nature, which condemns it as unknown to the law of the land.[39]

State courts often took the lead in developing new ideas about rights. In New York, for example, the high court articulated a broad conception of liberty in rejecting the authority of the state to prohibit cigar rolling in tenement houses. "Liberty," Judge Robert Earl contended, "in its broad sense as understood in this country, means the right, not only of freedom from actual servitude, imprisonment or restraint, but the right of one to use his faculties in all lawful ways, to live and work where he will, to earn his livelihood in any lawful calling, and to pursue any lawful trade or avocation."[40] In Kentucky, the state supreme court struck down a prohibition law, noting that "the question of what a man will drink, or eat, or wear, provided that the rights of others are not invaded, is one which addresses itself alone to the will of the citizen."[41]

Such arguments were not always successful, but they were increasingly voiced and taken seriously. In the Washington territory, a supreme court justice dissented from a ruling upholding the constitutionality of opium laws, arguing that such a law "relates purely to the private action or conduct of the individual."[42] In the U.S. Supreme Court, Justice Stephen Field dissented from the majority's decision that states could impose a maximum rate to be charged by owners of grain elevators, proclaiming that "if this is sound law . . . all property and all businesses in the State are held at the mercy of a majority of its legislature."[43] In the Michigan supreme court, a dissenting judge inveighed against the majority that upheld a state law authorizing "the sterilization of mentally defective persons." "There is a limit even to the power of the state over the bodies of men and women"; to say otherwise invites "atavism to the state of mind evidenced in Sparta, ancient Rome, and the Dark Ages, where individuality counted for naught against the mere animal breeding of human beings for purposes of the state or tribe."[44] In arguing against a state law prohibiting the advocacy of industrial sabotage or terrorism, Justice Louis Brandeis lectured his colleagues that those "who won our independence by revolution . . . did not fear political change" or "exalt order at the cost of liberty." The proper response to the advocacy of violence was "more speech, not enforced silence."[45]

Most cases involving rights during these decades came down to a conflict between the police powers of the state and the property rights of the individual (or business). During this period, the courts developed a more formal conception of the state police powers, the power to regulate social behavior in order to protect the health, safety, welfare, or morals of the community. When government exercises such powers, the interests of the individuals must give way. The crucial question for the courts was whether governments could properly claim the protection of the police powers to justify their actions. Again, Thomas Cooley helped establish the doctrinal framework.

> [I]f it assumes to be a police regulation, but deprives a party of the use of his property without regard to the public good, under the pretense of the preservation of health, when it is manifest that such is not the object and purpose of the regulation, it will be set aside as a clear and direct infringement of the right of property without any compensating advantages.[46]

Defending constitutional rights necessitated a judicial investigation of whether statutes were in fact pursuing legitimate objects and purposes. Making such determinations was often deeply controversial.

More often than not, the courts upheld legislative actions, but the times when they did not caused much consternation among politicians and activists. Perhaps the most infamous instance of a court invalidating legislation during these years was the U.S. Supreme Court's decision in

Lochner v. New York.[47] The case involved an increasingly common type of statute, a law imposing the maximum working hours on bakers (as well as a variety of public health regulations). The new regulation most seriously affected the numerous small bakeries manned by recent immigrants in and around the cities, and the law reflected the interests of several constituencies. Social reformers were increasingly effective in pushing governments to do something to improve the living and working conditions in the densely populated poor (and often immigrant) neighborhoods. Labor unions were successfully organizing and lobbying to benefit the economic conditions of workers. Large, mechanized bakeries were happy to reduce competition from small, labor-oriented bakeries. With only four state inspectors, the 1895 law was irregularly enforced, but unions were able to use it as leverage (one of the inspectors was himself an officer in the baker's union). The unions filed complaints with state officials against nonunion shops whose bakers worked overtime, but overlooked bakeries that agreed to unionize and illegally pay higher rates for the overtime hours.

Joseph Lochner himself reflected these complicated dynamics. A German immigrant, he had worked as a hired hand in bakeries before opening his own, where he and his wife worked with a small group of employees. As a shop owner, he had a contentious relationship with the local workers' union, and in 1902 a state inspector filed a criminal complaint against Lochner for allowing an employee to work more than forty hours in a week. The Master Bakers Association had resolved to test the law in court since they were not able to make much headway in revising the statute in the legislature, and Lochner and his long-time employee almost certainly cooperated to provide such a case. A narrowly divided state high court upheld the statute, but on appeal a divided U.S. Supreme Court struck it down. A majority of the justices concluded that protecting the public health was merely a pretext for a statutory provision that was really designed to give the favor of the state to a particular set of workers over their employers, violating the liberty of bakers to enter into labor contracts of their own choice. The primary dissent argued that the illegitimate purpose and effect of the act was not "beyond all question," and thus the courts should defer to the legislative judgment. But more famously, Justice Oliver Wendell Holmes penned a lone dissent ignoring the traditional police powers doctrine and accusing the court of reading its favored economic theories into the Constitution and interfering with the ability of popular majorities to make policy. "Every opinion becomes law," Holmes reflected, even if judges might sometimes find those opinions "novel and even shocking" or "if you like . . . tyrannical." So long as a "rational and fair man" would not admit that a law "infringe[d] fundamental principles as they have been understood by the traditions of our people and our law," then the judges should defer to the will of the legislature.

In 1905, the *Lochner* result was unusual, breaking from the court's general pattern of turning away constitutional challenges based on legislative abuses of the police powers and violations of due process. But over the next three decades such invalidations became somewhat more common, including laws prohibiting "yellow dog" (anti-union) employment contracts and female minimum wage laws. Progressive reformers ignored the more conventional dissent of Justice John M. Harlan and hailed the Holmes dissent as revealing the reality of judicial politics. *Lochner* rapidly became the symbol of conservative judicial activism on behalf of corporate interests.[48]

Like Holmes, many Progressives agitated for sharply curtailing the power of judicial review and questioned the value of constitutional rights. Former president Theodore Roosevelt called for a "pure democracy," in which the people would have the power to vote to overturn judicial decisions. Other reformers had their own ideas about how to rein in the courts, including proposals to prohibit judicial review or require unanimity on the court before a law could be invalidated. Meanwhile, conservative lawyers and politicians mobilized the American Bar Association and other outlets to defend the idea of a powerful, independent judiciary and popularize the belief that judicially protected rights were an important part of a republican government.

Due process cases might have been particularly controversial, but they did not constitute the bulk of the court's work when exercising the power of judicial review. More routine were cases involving the commerce clause, taxation powers, and government infringement on existing contracts. In deciding such cases, the federal judiciary embarked on a process of tearing down political barriers to the smooth functioning of a national economic market. The bulk of these judicial rulings were not particularly controversial, but helped establish the federal judiciary as a supervisory agent over the states. In the Gilded Age, as many state and local governments found themselves dramatically overextended (especially in the South), the federal courts blocked schemes by which governmental entities hoped to avoid paying their creditors. As railroads and corporations developed a national reach, the federal courts struck down state licensing requirements that only applied to out-of-state merchants or out-of-state goods, state rate caps on interstate railroad traffic, requirements that interstate rail traffic stop at all county seats, requirements that only meat from locally inspected livestock could be sold within a state, efforts to collect taxes on out-of-state sales, and efforts to prevent the importation of liquor into dry jurisdictions. Such decisions were often mundane, technical, and complicated, and often required delving into the unique details of a particular legislative scheme, but together they put states and localities on notice that they could not insulate themselves from national market forces.

The court spent less time enforcing constitutional limits on Congress, though some of its actions were significant and invited substantial criticism near the end of the nineteenth century. The justices inflamed the Populists when it struck down their favored federal income tax. Populist leaders denounced the income tax decision as the worst since *Dred Scott*, and were able to take control of the Democratic nomination convention in 1896. But the rise of the Populists within the Democratic Party merely solidified the Republican margin of victory in national races, and the income tax was not restored until a new generation of political leaders pursued a constitutional amendment in 1913. The court likewise gutted the Sherman Antitrust Act, insisting that the Congress could regulate goods in interstate commerce but not the manufacturing of goods that indirectly affected interstate commerce. Neither political party was terribly invested in a more expansive understanding of the commerce power at the end of the nineteenth century, but over the next three decades the federal government gradually pushed the boundaries of its regulatory powers outward, generally with the court's blessing. The most significant legal obstacle Congress encountered in those years was the Supreme Court's invalidation of the effort to ban the interstate shipment of goods made with child labor (which the court viewed as a transparent effort to regulate the manufacturing process).

Despite these interventions, the court mostly endorsed and aided the development of the administrative state and the expansion of government. As Congress tried to extend its own regulatory reach, the court gradually expanded the scope of the interstate commerce clause. Emphasizing that the power to regulate included the power to prohibit entirely, the court upheld various congressional bans on the movement of specified goods through interstate or foreign commerce, including lottery tickets, diseased cattle, colored margarine, films of prize fights, narcotics, prostitutes, and stolen cars. Accepting that the control of international borders and enforcement of international law are core rights of national sovereignty, the court accepted such controversial measures as the Chinese Exclusion Act, the federal prosecution and deportation of alien prostitutes, and the federal prosecution of the possession of counterfeit foreign currencies. The court raised no objection to such regulatory innovations as the creation of the Interstate Commerce Commission or the Food and Drug Administration or the imposition of an eight-hour workday on federal contractors and interstate carriers.

The cooperation between the federal judiciary and liberal reformers broke down in the 1930s. The crisis of the Great Depression and the political success of liberal Democrats gave rise to bold new state and federal measures to manage the economy during the New Deal. A bare majority of the justices on the Supreme Court strongly objected. The conservative "four horsemen," joined by the judicial centrists Owen Roberts and Charles Evans Hughes, struck down New Deal measures at an unprecedented rate during Franklin Roosevelt's first term, including such hallmark statutes as the National Industrial Recovery Act and the Agricultural Adjustment Act. New Dealers immediately introduced proposals in Congress to bring the court to heel, while the president took to the airwaves to castigate the conservative justices. After Roosevelt and his supporters won a decisive victory in the 1936 elections, Roosevelt proposed his "Court-packing" plan, which would have allowed him to immediately appoint a new justice for every sitting jurist over the age of seventy (potentially six new justices). Congress bogged down in a protracted battle over the bill, with conservative Democrats leading the opposition and public opinion sharply divided.

In March of 1937, the Supreme Court surrendered. Hughes and Roberts joined the liberals to uphold key statutes, and in the process reversed their own precedent on the constitutionality of the minimum wage. With the "switch in time," support for the court-packing plan dissipated, and the administration finally admitted defeat after the Senate majority leader's death in the summer of 1937. If the court's actions helped kill the court-packing bill, the evidence suggests that the swing justices had already decided to cast their support to the liberals before the court-packing plan was announced. The conservative justices likewise saw that they were defeated, and soon left the court, denouncing the judicial abandonment of the Constitution that they knew. There were no vacancies on the Supreme Court during Roosevelt's first term, but by the end of his second term Roosevelt had appointed five justices and eventually named a record-number of eight justices to the bench. Roosevelt-appointed justices wrote the landmark precedents of the late 1930s and 1940s that took the brakes off congressional power to pass the economic and social welfare legislation that it saw fit. Mulling the future of constitutional doctrine in this area, Justice (and former FDR attorney general) Robert Jackson concluded that in order for the reconstructed Court to strike down a federal regulation "the regulated activity would have to be so absurd that it would be laughed out of Congress." The remedy to objectionable statutes going forward was to be found "at the polls," not in the courthouse.[49]

V. A Rights Revolution

L iberals were divided over what the constitutional legacy of the New Deal should be. No one doubted that if the New Deal meant anything at all, it meant the expansion of state power. Politicians were to be empowered and entrusted to act for the public welfare. For some, influenced by the Progressives, the New Deal should mean the final victory of democracy over courts and the rejection of courts as "superlegislatures." Rights and courts were seen as inherently conservative and restrictive, and New Deal reform represented the victory of the people over the forces of reaction. Justice Felix Frankfurter and Judge Learned Hand best represented this school of thought, with Hand eventually wondering why the country should be ruled by a "bevy of Platonic guardians." For others, the New Deal should mean the triumph of liberalism over conservatism. The Lochner Court embodied conservative values and interests, and the success of the New Deal vanquished those interests and replaced them with liberal values and interests. Justice Robert Jackson and Justice William O. Douglas represented this school of thought, proclaiming the right "consciously to influence the evolutionary process of constitutional law, as other generations have done."[50] From this perspective, it is notable that the Roosevelt administration decided to advance a proposal that would have had the effect of taking over the court rather than prostrating the court.

What would a liberal-minded Court do with the power of judicial review? One obvious answer would be to get out of the way. Justice Harlan Stone, soon to be appointed chief justice by Roosevelt, asserted in 1938 that the courts should lean more heavily on the "presumption of constitutionality" and should uphold government regulations so long as they rested on "some rational basis."[51] Legislatures were to be given wide latitude to make the policies that they thought were in the best interest of the public. Consistent with the Progressive view of the Lochner era, the alternative was said to be judicial second-guessing of the wisdom and desirability of the law.

A less obvious answer would be to develop a new set of rights to be elaborated and enforced by the courts, even as old ideas about constitutional rights were abandoned. If the exercise of the police powers were to be subject only to a minimal rational basis review, at least in the context of property rights claims, then much of the constitutional jurisprudence of the first century and a half of the nation's experience was rendered obsolete. The courts replaced that jurisprudence with a new theory of preferred freedoms and multiple tiers of judicial scrutiny. At the same time that Justice Stone articulated the presumption of constitutionality for economic regulation, he posited in a famous footnote that the presumption might have a "narrower scope" in cases involving specific textual commitments, the processes of democracy, or particular "discrete and insular" minorities, such as religious groups, nationalities, or racial minorities. In such circumstances, "more exacting judicial scrutiny" might be warranted.[52]

Multiple tiers of judicial scrutiny were later formalized by the court. When reviewing the wartime detention of Japanese-Americans in internment camps, the court settled on a framework of "strict scrutiny" in cases of legislative restrictions employing "suspect classifications" based on race.[53] A majority of the justices found the restrictions justified in the case of national security, but over time the mere invocation of the standard was regarded as "strict in theory and fatal in fact."[54] Governmental restrictions on the basis of race or against "fundamental rights" had to meet a high bar in order to be upheld by the courts and could not claim the safe harbor of a presumption of constitutionality with its superficial judicial scrutiny. By the 1970s, the Court would carve out subcategories of "semi-suspect" government actions (such as those restricting individuals on the basis of their gender) that would draw a less-searching "intermediate" scrutiny.

Having committed itself to continued rights protection in cases involving Japanese internment, the Jehovah's Witnesses, and secular public-school activists, the judicial debate turned to which rights were to be deemed fundamental enough to be worthy of judicial protection. For justices like Felix Frankfurter, Benjamin Cardozo, and John Marshall Harlan II, the protected rights should be a narrow but flexible set of rights that were essential to a system of freedom and justice. Those rights protected against the state might well be different than those protected against the federal government by the Bill of Rights. For justices like Hugo Black, the protected rights should be carefully restricted to the set that were explicitly laid down in the text of the Constitution; the state and federal governments should be constrained by the same set of textually specified rights. Allowing judges to determine which rights might best balance progress with justice, Black worried, would invite a return to the Lochner era and the imposition of subjective judicial policy preferences. For many justices a bit more removed from the battles of the New Deal, the range of rights that might be regarded as "fundamental" could be safely expanded. In practice, this meant that when interpreting the requirements of the due process clause of the Fourteenth Amendment, the Court "incorporated" most of the particular requirements embodied in the federal Bill of Rights as constitutional limits on the states while also developing a fluid set of other "unenumerated rights" to restrict state governments. By the 1970s, the justices continued to debate on a case-by-case basis which particular right should be recognized, but the broader debate over whether that set was large or small was largely settled in favor of a large and growing set of protected liberties. As a result, many constitutional disputes were nationalized, as federal judges (more than state judges) vindicated numerous rights claims. Conservatives protested this federalization of local governmental disputes in the latter twentieth century, just as Progressives had complained about similar developments in the law in the early twentieth century.

The debates over incorporation and the identification of fundamental rights stretched across a range of cases and issues decided by the Warren Court. When the first Republican president since the Great Depression had the opportunity to appoint justices to the Supreme Court, he favored judicial moderates and liberals. For Dwight Eisenhower, the political and constitutional debates of the 1930s were ancient history that did not need to be revisited. As a consequence, a Court led by Eisenhower appointees Chief Justice Earl Warren (who had won bipartisan plaudits as a California politician) and Justice William Brennan (a Catholic Democrat, a constituency that Republicans were already courting in the 1950s) mustered majorities capable of launching a new rights revolution. A new generation of liberal justices appointed in the 1960s was more likely to embrace the label of judicial activism, rather than shy away from it. On issues like religious liberty, free speech, and racial equality, the justices readily agreed to remake the constitutional landscape by extending those protections in ways courts previously had not imagined doing. On issues like legislative apportionment, criminal justice, and sexual liberty, the court often moved boldly but had to overcome internal divisions to do so.[55]

The new constitutional law was not received quietly. The political reaction to the early Warren Court decisions in the 1950s set the tone. Those early political attacks were so severe that the court may well have slowed down in response. The 1954 school desegregation decision in *Brown v. Board of Education* launched Warren's tenure as chief justice. Criticism came immediately. Nearly every member of Congress from a southern state signed on to the 1956 Southern Manifesto denouncing the court for its "unwarranted exercise of power." Many state and local leaders heeded the call of Virginia Senator Harry Byrd for a campaign of "massive resistance" to the desegregation order. The lower federal courts were largely left to their own devices in developing plans to navigate between the integrationists and the segregationists. They gained moral support, though, from the president's decision to send troops to enforce a district judge's order to desegregate the Little Rock schools and the Supreme Court's subsequent pronouncement that the judiciary (not legislators or governors) was the "supreme" interpreter of the Constitution.[56] After the court decided a series of cases against anti-Communist laws in the mid-1950s, Congress came close to adopting a bill that would have stripped the Court of part of its appellate jurisdiction. Meanwhile, the anti-Communist John Birch Society sprinkled the landscape with "Impeach Earl Warren" billboards. The Court subsequently adopted a more deferential approach in Communist cases.

Criticism continued into the 1960s, but with less focused energy. When the Court declared that organized prayer in public schools was unconstitutional, many localities responded with quiet disobedience. When the Court announced that malapportioned legislatures violated constitutional equal protection requirements, legislators vocally objected—but the general public welcomed the decision. When the Court tightened constitutional protections for criminal defendants, police organizations and state judges complained but acquiesced. When the Court swept away long-established restraints on the media and public speakers, traditionalists grumbled but many welcomed the new literary and artistic license. The new rights agenda was part of a broader political agenda of liberal politicians. Congress and the executive in the 1960s adopted their own policies to advance some of these same goals, from school desegregation to voting rights. In other cases, political leaders helped encourage the courts to take action. Constitutional litigation was often advanced by interest groups with close ties to the liberal political establishment, such as the labor unions that agitated for legislative apportionment. The Johnson administration rewarded such efforts with offices as well as resources and praise, selecting the NAACP's Thurgood Marshall to be solicitor general and ultimately Supreme Court justice and Washington superlawyer Abe Fortas for the Supreme Court.

After a historic run (fortified by Felix Frankfurter's replacement in 1962 by Arthur Goldberg), the Warren Court reached an end in 1968. In the presidential race, Republican Richard Nixon and independent George Wallace repeatedly denounced the Warren Court in terms that harkened back directly to the Progressives and New Dealers. When he realized that Nixon was likely to win the White House, Warren met with President Lyndon Johnson to plan for his own retirement as soon as a new chief justice could be confirmed. Warren's plan to handpick his successor failed. His choice, Justice Abe Fortas, met a buzzsaw in the Senate confirmation hearings, where conservatives used the occasion to attack the overall record of the Warren Court. Embarrassed, the administration was forced to withdraw the nomination, and a year later Fortas was forced to resign from the court amidst a financial scandal. (Justice William O. Douglas resolved to ride out his own financial scandal, and short-lived impeachment threat, enabling him to reach his goal of becoming the longest serving justice.) As a result, Richard Nixon, Warren's old California rival, was able to name the next chief justice. Appellate court judge Warren Burger, a vocal critic of the Warren Court, got the nod. During his first term, Nixon was able to appoint four justices to the court, blunting the momentum of the Warren Court.

VI. JUDICIAL OSCILLATION

The departure of Warren and Fortas from the court in 1969 hobbled the liberal majority that had made a constitutional revolution over the course of the 1960s. Between 1969 and 1991, Republican presidents filled every vacancy on the Supreme Court, placing a total of ten justices on the bench. Since the conclusion of the Warren Court, Republican presidents have named every justice to join the bench save four. Republican appointees have held a majority of seats since 1970. But not all Republican appointees are the same. Two of Nixon's four nominees replaced Warren Court dissenters and had little effect on the overall composition of the court. Nixon and Ford were more focused on scoring political points than advancing legal objectives when making appointments. Most Republican presidents had to win judicial confirmation votes in Democratic Senates. The ideological orientation of the GOP had itself been reconstituted over the period, such that the critics of the Warren Court in the 1960s were not necessarily allied with the judicial conservatives of the 1990s.

Many predicted a counterrevolution from what was then known as the "Nixon Court." After Nixon's bitter attacks on the Warren Court and four appointments, many expected that the accomplishments of the Warren Court would soon be erased. The trajectory of constitutional law was more complicated than followers of Nixon's stump speeches would have forecast. William Brennan, the political general of the Warren Court, was able to continue to put together majority coalitions throughout the 1970s. Rather than rolling back the work of the Warren Court, the Burger Court overturned few of its predecessor's precedents. The justices instead chose a more modest path of blunting some of those earlier precedents by adjusting the inherited doctrine. At the same time, the early Burger Court handed down some startlingly liberal landmarks of its own.

The court since the Warren era has been defined by its centrists. During much of the Burger Court, Lewis Powell, Byron White, and Potter Stewart (nominated by Nixon, Kennedy, and Eisenhower, respectively) swung between liberal and conservative coalitions, anchored by William Brennan on one end and William Rehnquist on the other. During the Rehnquist Court, Sandra Day O'Connor and Anthony Kennedy played the role of swing voter, with Kennedy continuing in that role during the first years of the Roberts Court. Neither the conservative nor the liberal wings of the court have been able to claim reliable or robust majorities since the departure of Warren and Fortas destabilized the liberal majority that dominated the 1960s.

The dominance of the swing justice, and the fractured nature of the court, over the past few decades has left the court dependent on the inclinations of a handful of justices and with an unusually bipolar ideological profile. In the early years of the Burger Court, the justices issued such distinctly liberal decisions as the inclusion of obscenities in the freedom of speech (in an opinion written by Harlan), the limitation on the ability of the government to prevent publication of the Pentagon Papers (in a per curiam opinion), the extension of heightened scrutiny to classifications based on sex (in a Burger opinion), the abolition of the death penalty (in a per curiam), and recognition of abortion rights (in a Blackmun opinion). But the Burger Court soon began to issue more conservative decisions as well, such as the reestablishment of the death penalty (in a per curiam), the refusal to extend heightened scrutiny to policies that differentiate on the basis of wealth (in a Powell opinion), a loosening of constitutional protections for potentially obscene speech (in a Burger opinion), restricting the use of busing as a remedy for racially segregated schools (in a Burger opinion), the restriction of campaign finance regulations (in a per curiam decision), and the creation of exceptions to the application of the exclusionary rule for illegally obtained evidence (in a White opinion).

On the whole, the Burger Court moved in a more conservative direction on issues that were most central to the concerns of the Nixon administration, but continued to drift to the left elsewhere. Nixon cared about such hot-button political issues as criminal justice, school busing, and obscenity, and on those issues his appointments helped push constitutional law to the right by moderating earlier decisions. On other issues, such as women's rights, sexual liberty, and freedom of the press, the court reflected the broader, liberalizing currents of the time.

The actions of the Burger Court are also a reminder of the differences in the politics of the 1970s compared with those of the 1980s. Ronald Reagan might have borrowed (or shared) the tough-on-crime themes of earlier Republican presidential candidates from Barry Goldwater to Richard Nixon, but his coalition had more defined edges on a range of social issues that were still in flux when Nixon was trying to construct a Republican majority. Partisan and ideological positions on emerging cultural issues were not yet defined. Protestant evangelicals had not yet been integrated into the Republican coalition. When a fractured Court endorsed the use of affirmative action in college admissions in *University of California v. Bakke* in 1978, the justices heard from affirmative-action critics who thought they had been economically affected by the new policies, such as the American Federation of Teachers, the Fraternal Order of Police, and the American Jewish Committee. Affirmative-action supporters could still point to the innovations of the Nixon administration as key precedents for such policies. By contrast, when a polarized Court somewhat grudgingly reaffirmed the acceptability of the use of race in college admissions in a 2003 decision in *Grutter v. Bollinger*, the opposition to affirmative action was defined their ideological and partisan orientation rather than their economic self-interest. Affirmative-action critics in *Grutter* included a libertarian think tank, a conservative legal advocacy group, and the George W. Bush administration. When three of the four Nixon appointees joined the majority in *Roe v. Wade* in 1973, the justices mirrored the somewhat greater support at the time for abortion rights among Republican voters than among Democratic voters. When conservatives denounced as apostates the Reagan-Bush appointees who wrote the plurality opinion reaffirming abortion rights in *Planned Parenthood v. Casey* in 1992, they expressed the polarization of the two political parties into sharply divided pro-life and pro-choice camps.

Justice Anthony Kennedy's own record illustrates the split personality of the contemporary Court. Kennedy has been a classic swing justice. He has generally sat on a Court closely divided between stable liberal and conservative wings, and yet Kennedy himself has been willing to join either wing to form a majority coalition. As a result, he has often been the pivotal vote to invalidate a law. Like most modern justices, Kennedy shows little hesitation about intervening in political debates and striking down legislation. Moreover, like most modern justices on both the right and the left, Kennedy is committed to the judicial articulation and enforcement of a robust set of individual rights. Where Kennedy is unusual is that his vision of the preferred rights to protect partially overlaps with that of the conservatives and partially overlaps with that of the liberals. Justice Kennedy has written opinions for liberal majorities in free speech decisions (e.g., striking down channel-scrambling requirements for pornographic cable programming and restrictions on legal aid lawyers), homosexual rights decisions (e.g., striking down the criminalization of homosexual conduct and the federal ban on same-sex marriages), and criminal justice decisions (e.g., limiting the use of military tribunals and restricting the death penalty). He has been somewhat less likely to write for conservative majorities, but has provided the crucial fifth vote to the right wing of the court in cases on states' rights and federalism and campaign finance.

The vacillating Supreme Court of recent years has simultaneously offended, pleased, and worried both conservatives and liberals. Disappointed by their repeated losses on highly visible culture war issues such as abortion and sexual liberty, conservatives have continued their tendency since the Warren Court to criticize the "judicial activism" of the justices. Surprised by the willingness of the conservative justices to limit the ways in which Congress can restrict state governments and nullify hard-won campaign finance reforms, liberals have become more vocal in criticizing the Supreme Court. Even so, with a narrowly balanced Court, activists on both sides of the political aisle show trepidation over the possibility that judges might retreat from enforcing their favored constitutional values. During the conservative Justice Samuel Alito's confirmation hearings, pro-choice Senator Arlen Specter interrogated the nominee over whether the prospective justice was sufficiently committed to the inviolability of *Roe*. Conservative Senator Orrin Hatch was similarly concerned that future Justice Sonia Sotomayor might not feel due respect for the court's recent precedent extending the individual right to bear arms. Politicians, like the justices, preferred that the court be active in defending the rights they valued, and restrained when considering the rules that they did not.

Meanwhile, the court has proven willing to wade into a wide range of battles. The Warren Court laid the foundations. Shaking off Frankfurter's worries about entering the "political thicket," Justice Brennan redefined the traditional political question doctrine to conclude that constitutional challenges to how legislatures were apportioned were justiciable.[57] The court has shown little hesitancy since, whether evaluating how the House of Representatives exercised its impeachment power or establishing rules on how votes for presidential electors are to be counted.[58] The justices have been willing to intervene in other disputes as well. The courts had little to say about the basis and scope of executive privilege until it ruled on President Nixon's effort to withhold the Watergate tapes. To leave such matters to the executive and legislature, the Burger Court asserted, would be "contrary to the basic concept of separation of powers and . . . checks and balances."[59] Despite decades of politicians attesting that the judiciary could not answer the question of whether the legislative veto device was constitutional, the court sought to settle the matter in a 1983 ruling.[60] When Congress sought to exercise its authority under Section Five of the Fourteenth Amendment "to enforce" religious liberty by reestablishing a strict scrutiny standard for free-exercise claims, Justice Kennedy declared, "Congress does not enforce a constitutional right by changing what the right is." For Congress to disagree with the court's interpretation of the Constitution is to "alter" the Constitution.[61] Just as all roads led to Rome, the modern justices have generally believed that all constitutional controversies should lead to the court's own marble temple.

CONCLUSION

The practice of judicial review as we now know it was built over many years and by many hands. The relatively modest power that judges asserted in the early republic as part of their duty to resolve ordinary legal cases has become an important component of the American constitutional system. From Jeffersonians who hoped to correct the overreaching of the Federalist Party to abolitionists who hoped to control white southern legislatures to Gilded Age conservatives who hoped to maintain a check on mass democracy to modern liberals who hoped to vindicate the interests of unpopular constituencies, the idea of judicial review has been promoted and entrenched by wildly divergent groups with wildly divergent interests. What the supporters of judicial review have agreed upon over time is a distrust of unchecked political majorities, and judges have benefited from the diverse interests who have feared what life might be like as a political minority. Those diverse interests have disagreed about what the substance of constitutional law should be, but they have participated in a common project of building up a judiciary that will make and enforce an extensive web of constitutional law. As the institution of judicial review has been built, constitutional politics has shifted, often focusing on how to most effectively influence the judiciary rather than on how best to settle disputes outside the courts.

Suggestions for Further Reading

The literature on judicial review is vast and continues to grow at a rapid pace. Although much of the literature is concerned with normative theories about how judicial review should be exercised or empirical work on how the courts have employed the power of judicial review, the historical scholarship on the origins and development of the power of judicial review continues to be a robust area of exploration. The literature on constitutional politics is of a more recent origin, but it has grown rapidly as scholars have taken an interest not only in the normative and empirical issues surrounding political engagement with constitutional meaning but also with historical episodes of constitutional politics.

There are a number of short histories of the U.S. Supreme Court and the U.S. Constitution that focus on judicial review and the court's development of constitutional law. A fine one-volume survey of the court's history is Lucas A. Powe, Jr., *The Supreme Court and the American Elite, 1789–2008* (Cambridge: Harvard University Press, 2009). A classic but somewhat dated account can be found in Robert G. McCloskey, *The American Supreme Court*, revised by Sanford Levinson, 5th ed. (Chicago: University of Chicago Press, 2010). The multivolume and ongoing Oliver Wendell Holmes Devise History of the Supreme Court of the United States provides a valuable, more detailed history of the court. Charles Warren, *The Supreme Court in United States History*, 3 vols. (Boston: Little, Brown, 1923) is a classic history of the court's constitutional rulings in political context. Justin Crowe's *Building the Judiciary: Law, Courts, and the Politics of Institutional Development* (Princeton: Princeton University Press, 2012) examines the political organization and staffing of the federal judiciary. Alfred H. Kelly, Winfred Harbison, and Alfred H. Kelly, *The American Constitution: Its Origins and Development*, 7th ed., 2 vols. (New York: W. W. Norton, 1991) and David P. Currie, *The Constitution in the Supreme Court*, 2 vols. (Chicago: University of Chicago Press, 1992, 1994) provide detailed coverage of the history of constitutional law. Howard Gillman, Mark A. Graber, and Keith E. Whittington, *American Constitutionalism*, 2 vols. (New York: Oxford University Press, 2012) surveys American constitutional history in politics and law through excerpts of primary documents.

The modern normative debate over how judicial review should be exercised is often traced back to James Bradley Thayer, "The Origin and Scope of the American Doctrine of Constitutional Law," *Harvard Law Review* 7 (1893): 129. The argument over the antidemocratic and "countermajoritarian" nature of judicial review was given its characteristic, post-New-Deal form in Alexander M. Bickel, *The Least Dangerous Branch: The Supreme Court at the Bar of Politics* (Indianapolis: Bobbs-Merrill, 1962). The contemporary debate is well-represented by Ronald Dworkin, *Taking Rights Seriously* (Cambridge: Harvard University Press, 1978); Jeremy Waldron, *Law and Disagreement* (New York: Oxford University Press, 2001); John Hart Ely, *Democracy and Distrust: A Theory of Judicial Review* (Cambridge: Harvard University Press, 1980); Robert H. Bork, *The Tempting of America: The Political Seduction of the Law* (New York: Free Press, 1990); Keith E. Whittington, *Constitutional Interpretation: Textual Meaning, Original Intent, and Judicial Review* (Lawrence: University Press of Kansas, 1999); Larry D. Kramer, *The People Themselves: Popular Constitutionalism and Judicial Review* (Cambridge: Harvard University Press, 2005); Bruce A. Ackerman, *We the People: Foundations* (Cambridge: Harvard University Press, 1993); Cass R. Sunstein, *One Case at a Time: Judicial Minimalism on the Supreme Court* (Cambridge: Harvard University Press, 2001); Phillip Bobbitt, *Constitutional Fate: The Theory of the Constitution* (New York: Oxford University Press, 1982); Randy E. Barnett, *Restoring the Lost Constitution: The Presumption of Liberty* (Princeton: Princeton University Press, 2003).

A growing empirical and analytical literature has examined the behavior of judges as they exercise judicial review, and the opportunities for and constraints on judicial decision-making. Although much of this work has focused on the contemporary Supreme Court and treats judicial review as an abstraction, some of it focuses on more historically contextualized uses of judicial review. Useful introductions to that literature can be found in Robert A. Dahl, "Decision-Making in a Democracy: The Supreme Court as National Policy-Maker," *Journal of Public Law* 6 (1957): 279; Mark A. Graber, "The Nonmajoritarian Difficulty: Legislative Deference to the Judiciary," *Studies in American Political Development* 7 (1993): 35; Keith E. Whittington, *Political Foundations of Judicial Supremacy: The Presidency, the Supreme Court, and Constitutional Leadership in U.S. History* (Princeton: Princeton University Press, 2007); Tom S. Clark, *The Limits of Judicial Independence* (New York: Cambridge University Press, 2010); Gerald N. Rosenberg, *The Hollow Hope: Can Courts Bring About Social Change?*, rev. ed. (Chicago: University of Chicago Press, 2008); Lee Epstein and Jack Knight, *The Choices Justices Make* (Washington, DC: CQ Press, 1998);

Jeffrey A. Segal and Harold J. Spaeth, *The Supreme Court and the Attitudinal Model Revisited* (New York: Cambridge University Press, 2002).

The argument over the origins of judicial review is lengthy and was once politically salient. At the turn of the twentieth century, Progressive scholars debated whether the U.S. Supreme Court created the power of judicial review out of whole cloth or whether such a power had been anticipated by the founders. Edward S. Corwin did pioneering work on the early history of judicial review in works such as *The Doctrine of Judicial Review: Its Legal and Historical Basis* (Princeton: Princeton University Press, 1914); *The Basic Doctrine of American Constitutional Law* (Indianapolis: Bobbs-Merrill, 1914); and *The "Higher Law" Background of American Constitutional Law* (Ithaca: Cornell University Press, 1955). Other important early works included Charles Grove Haines, *The American Doctrine of Judicial Supremacy* (1914); Charles A. Beard, *The Supreme Court and the Constitution* (New York: Macmillan, 1912); Brinton Coxe, *An Essay on Judicial Power and Unconstitutional Legislation* (Philadelphia: Kay & Brothers, 1893); Louis B. Boudin, *Government by Judiciary*, 2 vols. (New York: William Godwin, 1932). More recent work has expanded this historical reconstruction of the early history of judicial review, generally reinforcing Corwin's argument that the initial exercise of the power of judicial review was well-grounded in the law and politics of the early republic. Particularly useful studies include William E. Nelson, *Marbury v. Madison: The Origins and Legacy of Judicial Review* (Lawrence: University Press of Kansas, 2000); Scott Douglas Gerber, *A Distinct Judicial Power: The Origins of an Independent Judiciary, 1606–1787* (New York: Oxford University Press, 2011); Philip Hamburger, *Law and Judicial Duty* (Cambridge: Harvard University Press, 2008); William Michael Treanor, "Judicial Review before *Marbury*," *Stanford Law Review* 58 (2005): 455; James O' Fallon, "*Marbury*," *Stanford Law Review* 44 (1992): 219; Mark A. Graber, "Establishing Judicial Review? *Schooner Peggy* and the Early Marshall Court," *Political Research Quarterly* 51 (1998): 221; William Van Alstyne, "A Critical Guide to *Marbury v. Madison*," *Duke Law Journal* 1969 (1969): 1; Mary Sarah Bilder, *The Transatlantic Constitution: Colonial Legal Culture and the Empire* (Cambridge: Harvard University Press, 2008); J. M. Sosin, *The Aristocracy of the Long Robe: The Origins of Judicial Review in America* (New York: Greenwood Press, 1989); and William Lowry Clinton, *Marbury v. Madison and Judicial Review* (Lawrence: University Press of Kansas, 1989).

Judicial review in the decades after the founding has traditionally received less attention from scholars, but some significant work has explored constitutionalism and the courts in these critical years. Larry Kramer's *The People Themselves: Popular Constitutionalism and Judicial*

Review (Cambridge: Harvard University Press, 2005) emphasized constitutional politics in the antebellum era as an alternative to judicial review. Similarly focusing on constitutionalism outside the courts during this period are studies such as Keith E. Whittington, *Constitutional Constructions: Divided Powers and Constitutional Meaning* (Cambridge: Harvard University Press, 1999); Gerald Leonard, *The Invention of Party Politics: Federalism, Popular Sovereignty, and Constitutional Development in Jacksonian Illinois* (Chapel Hill: University of North Carolina Press, 2002); William M. Wiecek, *The Sources of Antislavery Constitutionalism in America, 1760–1848* (Ithaca: Cornell University Press, 1977); David P. Currie, *The Constitution in Congress*, 4 vols. (Chicago: University of Chicago Press, 1999–2006); Laura J. Scalia, *America's Jeffersonian Experiment: Remaking State Constitutions, 1820–1850* (De Kalb: Northern Illinois University Press, 1999); Richard E. Ellis, *The Union at Risk: Jacksonian Democracy, States' Rights, and the Nullification Crisis* (New York: Oxford University Press, 1987); Gerald N. Magliocca, *Andrew Jackson and the Constitution: The Rise and Fall of Governmental Regimes* (Lawrence: University Press of Kansas, 2007); and Michael Kent Curtis, *Free Speech, "The People's Darling Privilege": Struggles for Freedom of Expression in American History* (Durham: Duke University Press, 2000). Other work has focused on the exercise of judicial review during this period, including extended studies of individual cases. Some notable work includes Mark A. Graber, "Federalist or Friends of Adams: The Marshall Court and Party Politics," *Studies in American Political Development* 12 (1998): 229; Mark A. Graber, "The Jacksonian Origins of Chase Court Activism," *Journal of Supreme Court History* 25 (2000): 17; Keith E. Whittington, "Judicial Review of Congress before the Civil War," *Georgetown Law Journal* 97 (2009): 1257; Richard E. Ellis, *Jeffersonian Crisis: Courts and Politics in the Young Republic* (New York: Oxford University Press, 1971); Mark R. Killenbeck, *M'Culloch v. Maryland: Securing a Nation* (Lawrence: University Press of Kansas, 2006); Kent R. Newmyer, *John Marshall and the Heroic Age of the Supreme Court* (Baton Rouge: Louisiana State University Press, 2002); Don E. Fehrenbacher, *The Dred Scott Case: Its Significance in American Law and Politics* (New York: Oxford University Press, 1978); Gerald Leonard, "Law and Politics Reconsidered: A New Constitutional History of *Dred Scott*," *Law and Social Inquiry* 34 (2009): 747; Harold M. Hyman and William M. Wiecek, *Equal Justice Under Law: Constitutional Development, 1835–1876* (New York: Harper & Row, 1982); C. Peter Magrath, *Yazoo: Law and Politics in the New Republic: The Case of Fletcher v. Peck* (New York: W. W. Norton, 1967); Stanley I. Kutler, *Privilege and Creative Destruction: The Charles River Bridge Case*

(Baltimore: Johns Hopkins University Press, 1989); and Jed Handelsman Shugerman, "Economic Crisis and the Rise of Judicial Elections and Judicial Review," *Harvard Law Review* 123 (2010): 1061.

The Civil War and Reconstruction were fertile years for constitutional politics and helped lay the foundation for a boom in the theory and practice of judicial review. The classic study of wartime constitutional concerns is James G. Randall, *Constitutional Problems under Lincoln* (New York: D. Appleton and Company, 1926). Robert M. Cover's article "The Origins of Judicial Activism in the Protection of Minorities," *Yale Law Journal* 91 (1982): 1287 pointed to the transformation in ideas about democracy and judicial review that the Civil War wrought. The Reconstruction Amendments were the culmination of a long effort to reconceptualize constitutional rights and provided an important new basis for the federal judicial review, as detailed in Bruce *Ackerman, We the People: Transformations* (Cambridge: Harvard University Press, 1998). Other useful works exploring the constitutional politics and law of this period include Pamela Brandwein, *Rethinking the Judicial Settlement of Reconstruction* (New York: Cambridge University Press, 2011); Daniel Farber, *Lincoln's Constitution* (Chicago: University of Chicago Press, 2003); Harold M. Hyman, *A More Perfect Union: The Impact of the Civil War and Reconstruction on the Constitution* (New York: Knopf, 1973); Stanley I. Kutler, *Judicial Power and Reconstruction Politics* (Chicago: University of Chicago Press, 1968); William E. Nelson, *The Fourteenth Amendment: From Political Principle to Judicial Doctrine* (Cambridge: Harvard University Press, 1988); Michael A. Ross, *Justice of Shattered Dreams: Samuel Freeman Miller and the Supreme Court during the Civil War Era* (Baton Rouge: Louisiana State University Press, 2003); Michael Kent Curtis, *No State Shall Abridge: The Fourteenth Amendment and the Bill of Rights* (Durham: Duke University Press, 1986); Jonathan Lurie, *The Slaughterhouse Cases: Regulation, Reconstruction, and the Fourteenth Amendment* (Lawrence: University Press of Kansas, 2003); Michael Vorenberg, *Final Freedom: The Civil War, the Abolition of Slavery, and the Thirteenth Amendment* (New York: Cambridge University Press, 2001); and Akhil Reed Amar, *The Bill or Rights: Creation and Reconstruction* (New Haven: Yale University Press, 1998).

The decades after Reconstruction witnessed a rebirth of judicial review as both state and federal courts became increasingly active in defining and enforcing the limits of government power and the scope of individual rights. New rights claims were advanced, even as the powers of government were reimagined and put to new uses. The Gilded Age and Progressive Era were long characterized as years dominated by an activist conservative

Supreme Court bent on advancing corporate interests at the expense of democratic majorities. This view of the constitutional jurisprudence of the period has undergone substantial revision in recent years, which has put greater emphasis on the support of the courts for government power, the extended roots of the doctrinal developments of the period, and the varied nature of the rights claims under consideration during the so-called *Lochner* era. The older literature is well-represented in such classic works as Arnold M. Paul, *Conservative Crisis and the Rule of Law: Attitudes of the Bench and Bar, 1887–1895* (Ithaca: Cornell University Press, 1960); Benjamin R. Twiss, *Lawyers and the Constitution: How Laissez Faire Came to the Supreme Court* (Princeton: Princeton University Press, 1942); Benjamin F. Wright, *The Growth of American Constitutional Law* (Boston: Houghton Mifflin, 1942); Carl B. Swisher, *American Constitutional Development* (Boston: Houghton Mifflin, 1943); and William F. Swindler, *Court and Constitution in the Twentieth Century*, 2 vols. (Indianapolis: Bobbs-Merrill, 1969–1974). Valuable more recent works include Michael Les Benedict, "Laissez-Faire and Liberty: A Re-Evaluation of the Meaning and Origins of Laissez-Faire Constitutionalism," *Law and History Review* 3 (1985): 293; Alan Jones, "Thomas M. Cooley and "Laissez-Faire Constitutionalism: A Reconsideration," *Journal of American History* 53 (1967): 751; Charles W. McCurdy, "Justice Field and the Jurisprudence of Government-Business Relations," *Journal of American History* 61 (1975): 970; Howard Gillman, *The Constitution Besieged: The Rise and Demise of Lochner Era Police Powers Jurisprudence* (Durham: Duke University Press, 1993); Hadley Arkes, *The Return of George Sutherland: Restoring a Jurisprudence of Natural Rights* (Princeton: Princeton University Press, 1994); Sarah Barringer Gordon, *The Mormon Question: Polygamy and Constitutional Conflict in Nineteenth-Century America* (Chapel Hill: University of North Carolina Press, 2002); Mark A. Graber, *Transforming Free Speech: The Ambiguous Legacy of Civil Libertarianism* (Berkeley: University of California Press, 1991); Charles A. Lofgren, *The Plessy Case: A Legal-Historical Interpretation* (New York: Oxford University Press, 1987); Paul L. Murphy, *World War I and the Origins of Civil Liberties in the United States* (New York: W. W. Norton, 1979); David M. Rabban, *Free Speech in Its Forgotten Years* (New York: Cambridge University Press, 1997); Linda Przybyszewski, *The Republic According to John Marshall Harlan* (Chapel Hill: University of North Carolina Press, 1999); Reva B. Siegel, "She the People: The Nineteenth Amendment, Sex Equality, Federalism, and the Family," *Harvard Law Review* 115 (2002): 947; Paul Kens, *Justice Stephen Fields: Shaping Liberty from the Gold Rush to the Gilded Age* (Lawrence: University Press of Kansas, 1997); William G. Ross, *A Muted Fury: Populists, Progressives, and Labor Unions Confront the Courts, 1890–1920* (Princeton: Princeton University Press, 1994); Stephen B. Wood, *Constitutional Politics in the Progressive Era: Child Labor and the Law* (Chicago: University of Chicago Press, 1968); James W. Ely, Jr., *The Guardian of Every Other Right: A Constitutional History of Property Rights*, 3rd ed. (New York: Oxford University Press, 2008); Ken I. Kersch, *Constructing Civil Liberties: Discontinuities and the Development of American Constitutional Law* (New York: Cambridge University Press, 2004); and Barry Friedman, *The Will of the People: How Public Opinion Has Influenced the Supreme Court and Shaped the Meaning of the Constitution* (New York: Farrar, Strauss, and Giroux, 2009).

The period since the New Deal has witnessed a dramatic transformation in constitutional law and the Supreme Court. The court retreated on some fronts, while aggressively expanding its activities in others. In the process, the substance of constitutional law was reconstructed. These events are nicely summarized in Richard C. Cortner, *The Supreme Court and the Second Bill of Rights: The Fourteenth Amendment and the Nationalization of Civil Liberties* (Madison: University of Wisconsin Press, 1981) and in Mark Tushnet, *The Rights Revolution in the Twentieth Century* (Washington, DC: American Historical Association, 2009). Other valuable studies include Barry Cushman, *Rethinking the New Deal Court: The Structure of a Constitutional Revolution* (New York: Oxford University Press, 1998); Risa Lauren Goluboff, *The Lost Promise of Civil Rights* (Cambridge: Harvard University Press, 2007); William E. Leuchtenburg, *The Supreme Court Reborn: The Constitutional Revolution in the Age of Roosevelt* (New York: Oxford University Press, 1995); Kevin J. McMahon, *Reconsidering Roosevelt on Race: How the Presidency Paved the Road to Brown* (Chicago: University of Chicago Press, 2003); Shawn Francis Peters, *Judging Jehovah's Witnesses: Religious Persecution and the Dawn of the Rights Revolution* (Lawrence: University Press of Kansas, 2000); Lucas A. Powe, Jr., *The Warren Court and American Politics* (Cambridge: Harvard University Press, 2000); Mark V. Tushnet, *Making Civil Rights Law: Thurgood Marshall and the Supreme Court, 1936–61* (New York: Oxford University Press, 1994); Clement E. Vose, *Caucasians Only: The Supreme Court, the NAACP, and the Restrictive Covenant Cases* (Berkeley: University of California Press, 1959); Michael J. Klarman, *From Jim Crow to Civil Rights: The Supreme Court and the Struggle for Civil Rights* (New York: Oxford University Press, 2004); Rebecca E. Zietlow, *Enforcing Equality: Congress, the Constitution, and the Protection of Individual Rights* (New York: New York University Press, 2006); Judith A. Baer, *Equality under the Constitution: Reclaiming the Fourteenth Amendment* (Ithaca: Cornell University Press, 1983); David J. Garrow, *Liberty and Sexuality: The Right to Privacy and the Making of Roe v. Wade* (Berkeley:

University of California Press, 1994); John D. Skrentny, *The Minority Rights Revolution* (Cambridge: Harvard University Press, 2004); and Louis Fisher, *Constitutional Conflicts between Congress and the President*, 5th ed. (Lawrence: University Press of Kansas, 2007).

Over recent decades, state and federal courts have continued to work out the legacy of the Warren Court. The mid-century Court provided an inheritance of revitalized judicial activism and a burgeoning array of civil liberties, but it also left behind controversy and uncertainty over how judges should use their powers and what rights should be protected. Conservatives and liberals have struggled with one another over how best to use tools wielded in the 1960s. The story is ongoing, but historically minded scholarship has already begun to explore judicial review and constitutional politics since the advent of the Burger Court. Valuable works include Kevin J. McMahon, *Nixon's Court: His Challenge to Judicial Liberalism and Its Political Consequences* (Chicago: University of Chicago Press, 2011); Donald Alexander Downs, *The New Politics of Pornography* (Chicago: University of Chicago Press, 1989); Reva B. Siegel, "Constitutional Culture, Social Movement Conflict and Constitutional Change: The Case of the de facto ERA," *California Law Review* 94 (2006): 1323; Johnathan G. O'Neill, *Originalism in American Law and Politics: A Constitutional History* (Baltimore: Johns Hopkins University Press, 2005); Richard A. Brisbin, Jr., *Justice Antonin Scalia and the Conservative Revival* (Baltimore: Johns Hopkins University Press, 1997); Scott Douglas Gerber, *First Principles: The Jurisprudence of Clarence Thomas* (New York: New York University Press, 1999); Howard Gillman, *The Votes that Counted: How the Court Decided the 2000 Presidential Election* (Chicago: University of Chicago Press, 2000); Thomas M. Keck, *The Most Activist Court in History: The Road to Modern Judicial Conservatism* (Chicago: University of Chicago Press, 2004); Earl M. Maltz, ed., *Rehnquist Justice: Understanding the Court Dynamic* (Lawrence: University Press of Kansas, 2003); Nancy Maveety, *Queen's Court: Judicial Power in the Rehnquist Era* (Lawrence: University Press of Kansas, 2008); Steven M. Teles, *The Rise of the Conservative Legal Movement: The Battle for the Control of the Law* (Princeton: Princeton University Press, 2008); Neal Devins, *Shaping Constitutional Values: Elected Government, the Supreme Court, and the Abortion Debate* (Baltimore: Johns Hopkins University Press, 1996); and Mark V. Tushnet, *A Court Divided: The Rehnquist Court and the Future of Constitutional Law* (New York: W. W. Norton, 2005).

The history of judicial review and constitutionalism in the states has not received its fair share of attention from scholars, but some recent works are beginning to fill in the gaps. Jed Handelsman Shugerman's *The People's Courts: Pursuing Judicial Independence in America* (Cambridge: Harvard University Press, 2012) provides an important starting point and overview.

Other valuable studies include Scott Douglas Gerber, *A Distinct Judicial Power: The Origins of an Independent Judiciary, 1606–1787* (New York: Oxford University Press, 2011); Daniel Joseph Hulseboch, *Constituting Empire: New York and the Transformation of Constitutionalism in the Atlantic World, 1664–1830* (Chapel Hill: University of North Carolina Press, 2005); Emily Zackin, *Looking for Rights in All the Wrong Places: Why State Constitutions Contain America's Positive Rights* (Princeton: Princeton University Press, 2013); G. Alan Tarr, *Understanding State Constitutions* (Princeton: Princeton University Press, 1998); Timothy S. Huebner, *The Southern Judicial Tradition: State Judges and Sectional Distinctiveness, 1790–1890* (Athens: University of Georgia Press, 1999); John J. Dinan, *The American State Constitutional Tradition* (Lawrence: University Press of Kansas, 2009); Donald S. Lutz, *The Origins of American Constitutionalism* (Baton Rouge: Louisiana State University Press, 1988); Willi Paul Adams, *The First American Constitutions: Republican Ideology and the Making of the State Constitutions in the Revolutionary Era*, Expanded Edition (Lanham, MD: Rowman & Littlefield, 2001); Marc W. Kruman, *Between Authority and Liberty: State Constitution-Making in Revolutionary America* (Chapel Hill: University of North Carolina Press, 1999); William E. Nelson, *Legalist Reformation: Law, Politics, and Ideology in New York, 1920–1980* (Chapel Hill: University of North Carolina Press, 2001); William J. Novak, *The People's Welfare: Law & Regulation in Nineteenth-Century America* (Chapel Hill: University of North Carolina, 1996); Mel A. Topf, *A Doubtful and Perilous Experiment: Advisory Opinions, State Constitutions, and Judicial Supremacy* (New York: Oxford University Press, 2011); Jeffrey M. Shaman, *Equality and Liberty in the Golden Age of State Constitutional Law* (New York: Oxford University Press, 2008).

Constitutional review has spread to many other countries of the world, although rarely in the same form as judicial review has taken in the United States. Some valuable works on the history and politics of constitutional review outside the United States include Diana Kapiszewski, Gordon Silverstein, and Robert A. Kagan, eds., *Consequential Courts: Judicial Roles in Global Perspective* (New York: Cambridge University Press, 2013); Georg Vanberg, *The Politics of Constitutional Review in Germany* (New York: Cambridge University Press, 2005); Alec Stone Sweet, *Governing with Judges: Constitutional Politics in Europe* (New York: Oxford University Press, 2000); Tom Ginsburg, *Judicial Review in New Democracies: Constitutional Courts in Asian Cases* (New York: Cambridge University Press, 2003); David Robertson, *The Judge as Political Theorist: Contemporary Constitutional Review* (Princeton: Princeton University Press, 2010); Ran Hirschl, *Towards Juristocracy: The Origins and Consequences of the New Constitu-*

tionalism (Cambridge, MA: Harvard University Press, 2004); Mark V. Tushnet, *Weak Courts, Strong Rights: Judicial Review and Social Welfare in Comparative Constitutional Law* (Princeton: Princeton University Press, 2008); David Erdos, *Delegating Rights Protections: The Rise of Bills of Rights in the Westminster World* (New York: Oxford University Press, 2010); and Gary J. Jacobsohn, *Apple of Gold: Constitutionalism in Israel and the United States* (Princeton: Princeton University Press, 1993).

ENDNOTES

1. Alexander Hamilton, James Madison, and John Jay, *The Federalist Papers*, ed. Clinton Rossiter (New York: New American Library, 1961), No. 78, 465.

2. Benjamin N. Cardozo, *The Nature of the Judicial Process* (New Haven: Yale University Press, 1921), 168.

3. Theodore Roosevelt, *Progressive Principles* (New York: Progressive National Service, 1913), 75; Learned Hand, *The Bill of Rights* (Cambridge: Harvard University Press, 1958), 73.

4. Jeremy Waldron, *Law and Disagreement* (New York: Oxford University Press, 2001).

5. The U.S. Constitution does give strong hints that something like judicial review would be exercised by state judges at least. The supremacy clause specifies that the Constitution, federal laws, and treaties "shall be the supreme law of the land; and the judges in every state shall be bound thereby, anything in the constitution or laws of any state to the contrary notwithstanding." State judges were expected to uphold federal constitutional requirements regardless of the directives of state legislatures. The clause had particular significance in making state judges implementers of federal treaty obligations.

6. *Marbury v. Madison*, 5 U.S. 137 (1803).

7. Bonham's Case, 8 Co. Rep. 114 (1610).

8. William Blackstone, *Blackstone's Commentaries*, ed. St. George Tucker, vol. 1 (Philadelphia: Birch and Small, 1803), 108.

9. Massachusetts Circular Letter, in Jedidiah Morse, *Annals of the American Revolution* (Hartford: n.p., 1824), 146.

10. Thomas Paine, *Rights of Man, Common Sense, and Other Political Writings*, ed. Mark Philip (New York: Oxford University Press, 1998), 122.

11. St. George Tucker, in *Blackstone's Commentaries*, 1:160.

12. Hamilton, et al., *Federalist Papers*, No. 48, 308.

13. James Madison, *Notes of the Debates in the Federal Convention of 1787* (New York: W. W. Norton, 1987), 304–306, 340–341.

14. *Caton v. Commonwealth*, 8 Va. 5 (1782).

15. James Iredell, *Life and Correspondence of James Iredell*, ed. Griffith J. McRee, vol. 2 (New York: D. Appleton and Company, 1858), 147.

16. Alexander Hamilton, *The Law Practice of Alexander Hamilton*, ed. Julius Goebel Jr., vol. 1 (New York: Columbia University Press, 1964), 377, 380.

17. *Hylton v. United States*, 3 U.S. 171 (1796).

18. *Vanhorne's Lessee v. Dorrance*, 2 U.S. 297 (1795).

19. *Hylton v. United States*, 3 U.S. 171 (1796); *United States v. The William*, 28 F.Cas. 614 (D. Mass. 1808); *United States v. Callender*, 25 F.Cas. 239 (C.C.D. Va. 1800); *Calder v. Bull*, 3 U.S. 386 (1798).

20. *Worcester v. Georgia*, 31 U.S. 515 (1832).

21. *Vanhorne's Lessee v. Dorrance*, 2 U.S. 297 (1795); *Calder v. Bull*, 3 U.S. 386 (1798).

22. *Beekman v. The Saratoga and Schenectady Railroad Company*, 3 Paige Ch. 45 (NY 1831); *Taylor v. Porter & Ford*, 4 Hill 140 (NY 1843).

23. *Wally's Heirs v. Kennedy*, 10 Tenn. 554, 556 (1831).

24. *Wynehamer v. People*, 2 Parker Crim. Rep. 490 (NY 1856).

25. 53 U.S. 299 (1852).

26. *Prigg v. Pennsylvania*, 41 U.S. 539 (1842).

27. *Jones v. Van Zandt*, 46 U.S. 215 (1847); *Ableman v. Booth*, 62 U.S. 506 (1858).

28. *Dred Scott v. Sandford*, 60 U.S. 394 (1857).

29. The majority disagreed about why Congress could not bar slavery in the territories, with Taney's opinion emphasizing the limited scope of the clause authorizing Congress to make needful rules for the territories and the concurring justices emphasizing the idea that the federal territories were held in trust for the common enjoyment of citizens from both the free and the slaveholding states.

30. It is commonly held that the court only struck down federal statutes in two cases prior to the Civil War, in *Marbury* and *Dred Scott*. I believe that this is mistaken, and that the court declared and enforced constitutional limits on congressional power in a score of (often low-profile) cases during those years. The cases are laid out in Keith E. Whittington, "Judicial Review of Congress Before the Civil War," *Georgetown Law Journal* 97 (2009): 1257.

31. See Gerald Leonard, *The Invention of Party Politics: Federalism, Popular Sovereignty, and Constitutional Development in Illinois* (Chapel Hill: University of North Carolina Press, 2002).

32. On the status of *McCulloch* before Reconstruction, see Mark A. Graber, "The Jacksonian Origins of Chase Court Activism," *Journal of Supreme Court History* 25 (2000): 17.

33. William Henry Harrison, Inaugural Address," in *A Compilation of the Messages and Papers of the Presidents*, ed. James D. Richardson, vol. 5 (New York: National Bureau of Literature, 1897), 1861.

34. Henry Clay, *Speech of The Honorable Henry Clay on the Subject of the Removal of the Deposits* (Washington, DC: Duff Green, 1834).

35. The Republicans were willing to do what was necessary to carve the western, pro-Union counties out of the seceding state of Virginia and creating a separate state of West Virginia in the midst of the war.

36. The Prize Cases, 67 U.S. 635, 670 (1862).

37. A majority of the justices on the U.S. Supreme Court initially suggested that the Reconstruction Amendments, and particularly the Fourteenth Amendment, would be limited to the context of slavery and race, but the minority's argument that the rights protected in those amendments extended to everyone won out in the end and set the stage for the rights-oriented jurisprudence of the next several decades. Slaughter-House Cases, 83 U.S. 36 (1873).

38. *Buchanan v. Warley*, 245 U.S. 60 (1917); *Corrigan v. Buckley*, 271 U.S. 323 (1926).

39. Thomas M. Cooley, *A Treatise on the Constitutional Limitations which Rest upon the Legislative Power of the States of the American Union*, 1st ed. (Boston: Little, Brown, 1868), 357.

40. In re Jacobs, 2 N.Y. Crim. R. 539 (1885).

41. *Commonwealth v. Campbell*, 133 Ky. 50 (1909).

42. *Territory v. Ah Lim*, 1 Wash. 156 (1890).

43. *Munn v. State of Illinois*, 94 U.S. 113 (1877).

44. *Smith v. Command*, 231 Mich. 409, 429 (1925).

45. *Whitney v. California*, 274 U.S. 357 (1927).

46. Cooley, 203.

47. 198 U.S. 45 (1905).

48. The scholarly assessment of *Lochner* has gone through substantial revision in recent years. Valuable recent works examining the case from a variety of perspectives can be found in Howard Gillman, *The Constitution Besieged: The Rise and Demise of Lochner Era Police Powers* (Durham, NC: Duke University Press, 1992); David E. Bernstein, *Rehabilitating Lochner: Defending Individual Rights against Progressive Reform* (Chicago: University of Chicago, 2011); Paul Kens, *Lochner v. New York: Economic Regulation on Trial* (Lawrence: University Press of Kansas, 1988).

49. Robert Jackson, "Memo on *Wickard*," in Howard Gillman, Mark A. Graber, and Keith Whittington, *American Constitutionalism*, vol. 1 (New York: Oxford University Press, 2013), 471.

50. Robert H. Jackson, *The Struggle for Judicial Supremacy* (New York: Vintage, 1941), xiv.

51. *United States v. Carolene Products*, 304 U.S. 144, 152 (1938).

52. Ibid., 152n4.

53. *Korematsu v. United States*, 323 U.S. 214 (1944).

54. Gerald Gunther, "In Search of Evolving Doctrine on a Changing Court: A Model for a Newer Equal Protection," *Harvard Law Review* 86 (1972): 8. In fact, the court's use of strict scrutiny has been complex, and sometimes less than fatal. See Adam Winkler, "Fatal in Theory and Strict in Fact: An Empirical Analysis of Strict Scrutiny in the Federal Courts," *Vanderbilt Law Review* 59 (2006): 793; Richard H. Fallon, Jr., "Strict Judicial Scrutiny," *UCLA Law Review* 54 (2006): 1267.

55. For details on the mid-century rights revolution, see Mark Tushnet, *The Rights Revolution in the Twentieth Century* (Washington, DC: American Historical Association, 2009).

56. *Cooper v. Aaron*, 358 U.S. 1, 18 (1958).

57. *Baker v. Carr*, 369 U.S. 186 (1962).

58. The notable exception has been legal challenges to the constitutionality of wars.

59. *United States v. Nixon*, 418 U.S. 683, 704 (1974).

60. *INS v. Chadha*, 462 U.S. 919 (1983). A legislative veto is a mechanism by which executive implementation of statutory authority can be blocked by a vote of a congressional committee, chamber, or whole.

61. *City of Boerne v. Flores*, 521 U.S. 507 (1997).